MIND

over

SPACE

By Nandor Fodor

ENCYCLOPEDIA OF PSYCHIC SCIENCE
THESE MYSTERIOUS PEOPLE
LAJOS PAP EXPERIMENTS
THE SEARCH FOR THE BELOVED
NEW APPROACHES TO DREAM INTERPRETATION
THE HAUNTED MIND
ON THE TRAIL OF THE POLTERGEIST

In collaboration with Hereward Carrington

HAUNTED PEOPLE

In collaboration with Frank Gaynor

FREUD: DICTIONARY OF THE UNCONSCIOUS

Nandor Fodor

MIND over SPACE

THE CITADEL PRESS • NEW YORK

FIRST EDITION

Library of Congress Catalog Card Number 62-8736
Manufactured in the United States of America
Published by The Citadel Press,
222 Park Avenue South
New York 3, New York

Contents

Introduction

THIS is a book for the Space Age.

For quite some time we have been able to send handwriting and photographs through space in seconds of time. Electronic scanning, however, does not move the original, it only copies it for a distant receiving station. Television is also based on image transmission. Movement and speech increases the illusion of reality to the point at which simultaneous television from several cities successfully imparts the grandeur of omnipresence to the viewing public.

To send an object instantaneously through space we need a further discovery: an electronic dissolution of matter at the sending station and a reassembling of the original form and composition at a distant point. From that discovery there may be just one step to the transmission through space of living things: plants, animals or – finally – human beings. Only in science fiction do we find this problem solved: by entering something like a telephone booth, the dispatcher sets the co-ordinates and the man of the future emerges from a similar receiving booth on the Moon or on a planet.

However, if human records, tradition and beliefs are to be attributed any value, another, non-mechanical way of traveling through space may exist: teleportation. It is a fascinating word, a fit companion to telepathy (feeling through distance) and telekinesis (moving distant objects without bodily contact). It is a form of human transportation: a sudden disappearance from a point in space and re-emergence elsewhere in a dazed condition, perhaps hundreds of miles away, as if waking from a state of trance. It has been reported from the beginnings of human history. In the Bible it is accomplished by the Spirit of the Lord. In mythology, magic, witchcraft, fairy lore and spiritualism the spiritus rector appears in a variety of guises, and in the present day our speculative approach is bolstered by a possible interaction with the fourth dimension.

This book is a monograph of data gathered from ancient and modern records by patient research. It is fairly exhaustive and is not inspired by the spirit of debunking, rather with a view that the human mind may have capabilities the limits of which we do not suspect. Let the reader determine for himself whether unknown electro-magnetic powers may exist on the organismic level of the human psyche (or at the heart of all living things), and whether in exceptional conditions and in exceptional organisms such powers may manifest themselves in our own days, tendering the vision that in generations to come they may be available for development and control for the benefit of the whole human race.

NANDOR FODOR

◂ CHAPTER I ▸

Taken Up by the Lord

ONE of the most intriguing forms of psychic phenomena is the transportation of human beings, animals and inanimate objects, often over great distances, in a fraction of the time it would take to cover the same distances by normal means. It is as though the barriers of space-time somehow are transcended.

This paranormal transportation – known as teleportation – undoubtedly occurred throughout human history, as indicated by certain curious myths and legends of earliest times and by well-documented reports of the present. For as long as it has occurred men have groped for an explanation. What agency possibly could effect, in literally the twinkling of an eye, the disappearance of a man from one location and his reappearance at another? Are supernatural powers, or some natural but unknown power of the human mind by which it can act on space, responsible?

Men base their theories on the knowledge or beliefs they possess at any particular time. At different periods gods, demons, sorcerers, witches, fairies and ghosts have been advanced as the cause.

In the Bible, which is considered to have a historical foundation, we find accounts of a miracle known as Translation into Heaven by the Spirit of the Lord. The most dramatic of such accounts is the one describing the prophet Elijah's disappearance from mortal view in a chariot of fire.

> And it came to pass, as they still went on, and talked, that, behold, there appeared a chariot of fire, and horses of fire, and parted them both asunder; and Elijah went up by a whirlwind into heaven. (II Kings 2, 1.)

Few passages in the Old Testament equal in drama the description of this momentous event. Moreover, the Biblical record is supported by testimonies that will stand critical examination.

Elisha, the principal witness, was prepared for the event. He knew that he was walking with his master for the last time. So did many others, "the sons of the Prophet that were at Bethel."

They came to meet him and asked him: "Knowest thou that the Lord will take away thy master from thy head today?" He answered them: "Yea, I know it; hold ye your peace!"

The same question was addressed to him by "the sons of the Prophet that were at Jericho," and he returned the same answer. Because he knew that the supreme moment of his master was coming, Elisha was determined to stay with him.

Followed from afar by 50 pairs of anxious eyes, Elijah performed his last miracle by smiting the waters of the Jordan with his mantle. The waters divided and Elijah and Elisha crossed on dry ground.

Elijah's hour was now at hand. He turned to Elisha and said: "Ask what I shall do for thee before I be taken away from thee." Elisha asked that a double portion of Elijah's spirit should rest upon him.

Elijah said: "Thou hast asked a hard thing; nevertheless, if thou see me when I am taken from thee, it shall be so unto thee; but if not it shall not be so."

Elijah's disappearance thus was made the crucial test of Elisha's seership. He would inherit a double portion of Elijah's spirit if he were to see how he vanished. Prophets have been moved through space before by the spirit of the Lord, but no one yet had seen the actual means by which their transportation was accomplished. Elisha saw it and he cried: "My father, my father, the chariot of Israel, and the horsemen thereof."

As Elijah never was seen again the fact is established that he was whirled away by some mysterious power. The appearance of the chariot of fire as a means of his transportation rests on Elisha's testimony alone.

Elijah's mantle fell from him as he disappeared. Elisha took it and wore it. With it, as predicted, Elijah's power descended on him. He divided the waters of the Jordan as Elijah had done. The Sons of the Prophet at Jericho, seeing him alone, bowed to the ground before him and accepted him as Elijah's successor.

But while Elisha was convinced that Elijah had ascended bodily to heaven, the Sons of the Prophet had their doubts. They did not see the chariot of fire. They were certain only that Elijah was dead. They thought that his body might be found and insisted on a search of the countryside "lest peradventure the Spirit of the Lord hath taken him up, and cast him upon some mountain, or into some valley."

It was not for the first time that Elijah was carried away. If he died in the process, they thought, his body must have dropped somewhere. Elisha disagreed because he saw the chariot of Israel and knew that this was not just another mysterious disappearance.

Jehovah, in the Hebrew ideology of the times, lived in a fiery element and had horses and chariots at His disposal. If His chariot descended, Elijah must have been taken into His presence and therefore would be seen no more.

The Sons of the Prophet searched for three days. They found nothing. Let us, therefore, assume that Elijah's body was not to be found. Are we to accept Elisha's testimony that it was taken away in a chariot of fire?

What was it Elisha saw? What was his state of mind when he saw it?

That his mind was predisposed to a vision of a chariot of fire by Hebrew ideology and by his foreknowledge of Elijah's impending death seems unquestionable. It also may be taken for granted that Elijah's farewell words acted as a powerful suggestion. Elisha's future as a prophet hung in the balance. If he failed to see how Elijah was taken away, Elijah's power would not descend on him. Picture him overwrought, grief-stricken over the impending loss of his master, anxious over his own future!

In that state of mind the drama of Elijah's disappearance would have caused an abnormal awareness in any ordinary mortal. Was it not likely that in Elisha's unconscious the idea of the chariot of fire as the only fitting vehicle for the last journey of the prophet from earth to heaven already was taking visual shape? Subjectively he was all prepared for an overwhelming visual experience.

A blaze of light enveloped Elijah — and he vanished. It may be expected that the emotional shock projected Elisha's dominant mental ideas into visual form. The blaze of light actually assumed for him the shape of a chariot and horses.

But was there a blaze of light? Records of similar disappearances throughout the centuries indicate that the vortex of power that appears to accomplish the stupendous feat of human transportation does sometimes produce a luminous phenomenon which may give the impression of fire. From fire to fiery chariot is a mere step. It matters little whether the luminous phenomenon was objective or subjective. Elisha witnessed a tremendous event when his master vanished and could not but conclude that he saw Elijah ascend to heaven.

The 50 Sons of the Prophet had only their previous experiences to go by. It was a matter of common knowledge to them that Elijah, from time to time, was carried away by the Spirit of the Lord and that his body never came to harm.

Not so long before, Elijah predicted a bad drought. When it came to pass he was held responsible for it. King Ahab, in his anxiety to preserve the horses on which his army depended, was on the march. Obadiah, his steward, passed through the land in another direction. Suddenly he found himself face to face with Elijah. He knew that he had to report the finding of the prophet to his king, but he knew also that unless he could produce Elijah in person Ahab would have him killed.

Elijah promised that he would call on the king, but Obadiah wanted to know what would happen if "it will come to pass, as soon as I am gone from thee, that the Spirit of the Lord will carry thee whither I know not." Then Elijah assured him: "As the Lord of the Hosts lives, before whom I stand, I shall surely show myself unto him today."

Did he know that the Spirit of the Lord would have no power over him that day, or that it could not carry him away against his will?

Beyond the crude notion of the chariot of fire, the Bible gives us no hint of the dynamics or the purpose of these aerial transportations. They seem to have been spontaneous occurrences, without intelligent design. The Spirit of the Lord could not be questioned, doubted or resisted. No harm was known to result from these mysterious journeys unless translation to heaven was a subsequent invention to cover up transportation into a faraway land from which there was no return. It was possible to assume, as did the Sons of the Prophet, that an accident had occurred. But assuming there was no accident, we still do not know what it means to be translated to heaven; and the Bible is not too helpful.

> By faith Enoch was translated that he should not see death and was not found, because God had translated him; for before his translation he had this testimony that he pleased God. (Hebrews 11, 5.)

The words "was not found" indicate that a search was made for his body as in the case of Elijah and that the searchers concluded that he was translated because they failed to find him.

In one instance we can calculate accurately the distance of transportation. It is in Acts 8:

> 39. And when they were come up out of the water, the Spirit of the Lord caught away Philip, that the eunuch saw him no more; and he went on his way rejoicing.
>
> 40. But Philip was found at Azotus; and passing through he preached in all the cities, till he came to Caesarea.

The eunuch rejoiced because he saw a miracle: the vanishing of Philip. One moment he was there, in Gaza,* on the water's edge, and the next he was gone, reappearing at Azotus 30 miles away. The description that he was "found" faintly suggests that he appeared dazed and not

*The desert of Gaza once again became the scene of transportation in monachistic history. Four monks of Hilarion, the founder of monachism in Palestine, were on their way in the desert of Gaza to their convent at Bethelea when, according to Sozomen, Malchio, the youngest and most esteemed of the four, suddenly vanished from their midst, and later in the journey reappeared. *(Eccl. Hist. Lib.* VI. c. 32.)

quite himself — a recurrent feature, as we shall see, in all similar mysteries.

For a rational motive behind transportation we must turn to the Apocrypha. In Bel and Dagon we read:

> 33. Now there was in Jewry the prophet Habakkuk, who made pottage, and had broken bread into a bowl, and was going into the field, for to bring it to the reapers.
> 34. But the Angel of the Lord said to Habakkuk, go carry the dinner that thou hast into Babylon unto Daniel, in the lion's den.
> 35. And Habakkuk said, Lord, I never saw Babylon; neither do I know where the den is.
> 36. Then the Angel of the Lord took him by the crown and lifted him up by the hair of his head, and with the blast of his breath set him in Babylon over the den.
> 37. And Habakkuk cried, saying, Oh, Daniel, Daniel, take the dinner which God has sent thee.
> 38. And Daniel said, Thou has remembered me, Oh God; neither hast Thou forsaken them that love Thee.
> 39. So Daniel arose and did eat; and the Angel of God set Habakkuk in his own place again immediately.

The word "immediately" should be noted. The Angel of the Lord accomplished Habakkuk's transportation from Judea to Chaldea "with the blast of his breath." It also is worth noting that Habakkuk did not land on solid earth in Babylon. He apparently hovered over the lion's den, dropped the food and watched Daniel eat. Lifting by the hair of the head probably is allegorical and indicates only the ease with which the feat was accomplished, or hints at the presumed lightness of Habakkuk's body.

While Habakkuk heard a voice and felt a touch on his forehead, Ezekiel in trance (the hand of the Lord fell upon him) saw a luminous apparition which "put forth the form of a hand and took me by a lock of mine head;

and the spirit lifted me up between the earth and the heaven, and brought me in the vision of God to Jerusalem, to the door of the inner gate that looketh eastward towards the North."

But for the lock of his head, the experience could be called a subjective one, as on the occasion when the spirit took him up and he heard a voice of great rushing, saying, "Blessed be the glory of the Lord from His place," the noise of wings of the living creatures that touched one another and the noise of the wheels over against them. The recorders are uncertain as to what actually took place. When at times the spirit of the Lord began to move young Samson in the camp we may doubt the objectiveness of the event. But we do not find such doubts openly stated until we read St. Paul (Cor. XII. 2). He knew a man in Christ who was "caught up to the third heaven" and "heard unspeakable words which it is not lawful for man to utter." But he could not tell "whether in the body or out of the body; God knoweth." The wording suggests that St. Paul considered it equally possible that the experience was subjective and that it was objective, in which case it would fall under the heading of transportation mysteries.

Enoch was translated that he should not see death. Moses failed to earn the same privilege.

> The Lord buried him in a valley in the land of Moab, over against Beth-peor; but no man knoweth his sepulchre unto this day. (Deut. 34. 6.)

As Moses died on the top of Pisgah, "burying by the Lord" is just another expression for vanishing without a trace. According to an old legend preserved by Josephus* he was talking on a mountain with Joshua, the general,

***Antiquities*, Book IV, Chapter VIII, Section 48.

and Eleazer, the high priest, when a cloud obscured him. He vanished and never was seen again.

In the disappearance of the body of Jesus from the rock-hewn tomb we face a better attested mystery. The body vanished. The shroud fell from it as the mantle fell from Elijah. But in this case no search of the surrounding mountains and valleys was made as the immediate apparition of Jesus in the garden gave rise to a belief in bodily resurrection with which the vanishing of his mortal remains fitted well.

The body was placed in the tomb Friday night. Its disappearance was not noticed until Sunday morning. There is no hint in the Bible as to how and when it may have gone. But if the Shroud of Turin is a genuine relic, as Catholics claim, the experiments of Dr. Paul Vignon, Professor of Biology at the Institute Catholique, Paris, would indicate that it disappeared almost immediately after the sepulchre had been closed by a stone.

In several cases of transportation recorded in Ethiopic manuscripts the Virgin Mary takes the place of the Spirit of the Lord.*

> She transported a sick monk to Jerusalem and back to his deathbed (p. 33). She carried a chaste abbot to Heaven in the body (p. 303) and she transported the church of the monastery of Akona, monks and all, to the edge of a stream where it should have been built.

While this story need not be considered anything more than folklore, the monumental nature of the feat is paralleled by two curious details: the monks were exceedingly numerous and they all were fast asleep. Had there been any indication that their sleep was not a nat-

*Sir. E. A. Wallis Budge: *One Hundred and Ten Miracles of Our Lady Mary,* Oxford University Press, London, 1933.

ural one but a state of trance, for a concerted output of "power," the story might have been considered a record of a psychic mystery.

◂ CHAPTER II ▸

Traveling by Magic

TRANSLATION to Heaven always is a final consummation of an exceptional life. It is a one-way journey and endures for eternity. The main difference between translation and transportation is that the latter term covers distances on this earth; translation leads to another realm of existence and writes finis to the tale.

Where the religious element is absent, in place of the Spirit of the Lord we find the magic or mythology of the pre-Christian era or other "unhallowed" agencies of the post-Christian centuries. The chariot of fire changes into a fire-spitting dragon to help Medea escape from the consequences of her evil deeds. Daughter of Aetes, King of Colchis, this sorceress with whose help Jason captured the Golden Fleece, killed two of her own children and escaped from Jason's vengeance "through the air upon a chariot drawn by winged dragons." Later she attempted to poison Theseus. Again "to avoid punishment which her wickedness deserved, she mounted her fiery chariot and disappeared through the air."*

When Ganymedes of Phrygia disappeared from Mount Ida, where he was hunting or tending his father's flocks (to become the cup-bearer of the Gods), "he was carried away by an eagle to satisfy the unnatural desires of Jupiter."** However crudely put, the myth at least reveals a libidinal need behind transportation, a need displayed

*Lempriere, *Classical Dictionary,* page 280.
***Ibid.*

later by the Fairy Queen in capturing mortals and keeping them prisoners of Fairyland.

The Church must be wrong in recognizing only religious need behind transportation. Moreover, a Catholic definition of religious need may differ considerably from a heathen one. Consider Abaris, the Scythian, son of Seuthes, a priest of Apollo. He was called an "aethrobat" or air-walker. By the help of a flying arrow which he received as a gift from Apollo he gave oracles and transported himself wherever he pleased. The mixture of magic and religion which his case represents is typical of the pre-Christian era, which he preceded by about 500 years.

While Abaris is rather a legendary character, we know more about his great contemporary, Pythagoras, who left his mark on science and philosophy. According to Porphyry's biography, Pythagoras was "on one and the same day at Metapontum in Italy and at Tauromenium in Sicily, and conversed with his friends in both places." Abaris may have experienced levitation only, but this clearly suggests transportation, whether magic, science, or a psychic disposition is to be credited for the feat.

The Christian church, in its first attempts to monopolize miracles, became very fond of calling dissidents sorcerers if they exhibited unusual powers. So we find Simon Magus, the first heretic of the Christian era, described as a sorcerer who bewitched the people of Samaria into believing him to be "the Great Power of God." (Acts, VIII. 5.) Part of his sorcery was his alleged ability to make himself invisible, to pass through rocks and mountains without hindrance, and to fly in the air.

According to Clemens Simon Magus died at Rome during a contest with Peter. He levitated to a great height, but Peter prayed and Simon Magus fell down to his death – a rare instance of fatality among thaumaturges. His tragic end was considered proof that sorcery or the devil's work cannot stand up against divine grace – a cry that echoed down the centuries against all miracle workers who were not devout Christians.

According to G. R. S. Mead* Simon is grossly misinterpreted by his orthodox opponents. He was the originator of "those systems of religio-philosophy and theosophy which now are somewhat inaccurately classed together under the heading of Gnosticism." As to his miracles, Mead considers them to be in the domain of legend and not history. Nevertheless he states:

"The legends of magic are the same in all countries, fantastic enough to us in the 19th century, in all conscience and most probably exaggerated out of all correct resemblance to facts by the excited imagination of the legend-tellers, but still it is not all imagination, and after sifting out even 99 percent of rubbish, the residue that remains is such vast evidence to the main facts that it is fairly overwhelming, and deserves the investigation of every honest student."**

We thus may place Simon Magus at the top of the list of people who, in contradistinction to those caught up by the Spirit of the Lord, are said by the Church to have been transported by the Devil – looking after his own.

Around the end of the first century of the Christian era we meet with the last famous pagan philosopher and thaumaturge, Apollonius of Tyana, whose life story, written by Flavius Philostratus within 100 years of his death, has been the subject of considerable literary controversy. The work was commissioned by Domina Julia,

---

*G. R. S. Mead, *Simon Magus*, London, 1892.
**Ibid, page 89.

the mother of Caracalla and the wife of Septimus Severus. To gather his material, Philostratus visited the cities where Apollonius lived, collected testimonials, examined letters by Apollonius in possession of Emperor Hadrian, and procured detailed information from notebooks of Damis, the chief disciple of Apollonius. The book was published in 216 A.D. in Greek. The only English translation is Rev. E. Berwick's work which, according to Mead, "in most places gives us a paraphrase rather than a translation and frequently mistakes the meaning."

The most debated incident is the trial of Apollonius before the tyrant Domitian. He is said to have vanished from the imperial presence before a number of people, about midday, and to have appeared in the evening of the same day before Demetrius and Damis in Puteoli, which was about three days journey from Rome.

The evidence for the vanishing is doubtful, even according to Philostratus, but the experience of the disciples is worthy of consideration. It appears that, as in the case of Jesus on the road to Emmaus, he was not recognized although he walked and conversed with them. "When he discovered himself to them, he stretched out his hand, asked them to accept and examine it, and determine whether he was merely an apparition or a reality, for — said he — 'if I bear being touched, you must be persuaded that I am alive, and that to reach here I made use of neither the ram of Phryxus nor the wings of Daedalus.' He then recounted to them minutely the story of his defense that they might relate every circumstance to Telesinus, who never ceased making inquiries."

A second story of the transportation of Apollonius is described by Philostratus in these words: "The plague was now raging in Ephesus, and no remedy was discovered that could check its progress, and on which account ambassadors came to Apollonius entreating him to come as their physician and undertake the cure. When he heard this he said, 'I think the journey is not to be delayed;' and no sooner had he uttered the words than he was at Ephesus, like Pythagoras who showed himself at one and the same time in Thurium and Metapontum."

Here is a new urge behind transportation, that of the physician to preserve human life, but the record hardly can be called satisfactory. It may speak only of simultaneous appearance which Catholic students of miracles call ubiquity or bilocation, psychical researchers the projection of the double. Only by the lack of mention of Apollonius' subsequent disappearance, as a phantom dissolving into mist, i.e., by the negative of the picture, does the account qualify as transportation.

In the trial of Apollonius before the court of Domitian we find the disappearance and his appearance before the disciples connected, but this picture is distorted by the unaccounted time lag between midday and the evening hours. Not being recognized by Damis and Demetrius as he walked and talked with them, we may query whether Apollonius was quite himself, or mentally still bewildered, perhaps not quite out of trance, only recovering when he made his identity known to the others.*

The majority of the records establish as fact that transportation is not under conscious control. In ascribing the power to the Spirit of the Lord the Bible acknowledges the same. The claim that the great thaumaturges could vanish at will must be a legendary addition to

*That Apollonius did learn something from the Brahmins on a visit to India, we find clearly indicated in Book III, Chapter XV of Philostratus' work in the following words: The Brahmins, after ritual cleansing, "made a ring and formed a choir which Iarchas led, and they struck the ground with their rods; and the earth swelled like waves, and they were raised two cubits above the ground. Meanwhile they sang a chant like the paean of Sophocles which is sung in Athens in honor of Aesculapius."

ancient records. Elijah, in one instance, seemed to be able to assure himself against involuntary disappearance, but this exception does not effect the essential spontaneity of the phenomenon. Simon Magus is credited with a greater range of powers than Elijah, but this is contradicted by his tragic end. Yet we find the basic elements of transportation present when his ability to disappear and pass through rocky barriers is mentioned. It was during a levitation and not a transportation demonstration that he fell to his death.

Transportation is instantaneous and unseen. Levitation is a spectacle, whether the ascent is close to the ground or exceptionally high as Simon's and, 12 to 13 centuries later, of Princess Agnes of Bohemia (1205-1281) and of the Flemish Coleta, Abbess of Ghent (1381-1447), whose bodies were lifted out of sight into the clouds. Levitation is not an initial phenomenon to transportation, as in all classical cases the body disappears from the ground in a split second. Levitation only runs counter to gravitation; transportation runs counter to our accepted concepts of space.

Hence, when King Solomon is said (by the author of the Arabic book *Tarikh-mon-Te-Kheb*) to have been carried on the back of a Jinn to distant places, when Zoroaster is said to have crashed into the King's presence by cleaving the roof of the palace (Howitt: *History of the Supernatural,* Vol. I, page 268), we have fragments but not the picture of transportation itself.

The fiery chariot of Elijah, the fire-spitting dragon, the flying arrow of Abaris, the chariot of doves or swans of Aphrodyte, the ram of Phryxus in the legend of the Golden Fleece, the beast of Mohammed, the golden sandals of Hermes, the ring of Gyges, the wings of angels, the magic carpet, the magic word or the stone of invisibility that Hubert, Earl of Kent, was accused of having stolen from the King's Jewel House in 1233,* are frail, pictorial and verbal attempts to bring a mystery closer to contemporary understanding.

Caught up by the Spirit of the Lord, as told in the Bible, is by far the clearest and best metaphysical explanation even though it sheds no light on the physical nature of the feat. The substitution of the Devil as the agency in non-Catholic circles is a theological prevarication. No church can monopolize the Spirit of the Lord and all living things must equally share in it. The power must be the same whether it is used by witches to reach the Sabbath, by savages to perform magical errands, by fairies to kidnap human beings, or by the spirits of the dead to convince the world of the truth of Spiritualism. Only the unconscious needs and the explanations of the agency vary.

In order that the clarity of the picture should not be obscured by legendary interpolations, it is now necessary to give a summary of all the classical features of transportation, with a mental reservation for exceptions and variations:

1. The phenomenon is unexpected, unwanted and unpreventable.

2. The transported person disappears from sight without warning.

3. The disappearance or reappearance may take place amidst luminous or cloud-like phenomena.

4. At the moment of disappearance consciousness is lost and a state of amnesia prevails when consciousness returns at a distant place.

5. The appearance elsewhere is instantaneous.

*Montague Summers: *Discovery of Witches,* page 8.

6. The destination is a random one.

7. The phenomenon serves no intelligible purpose.

8. It causes no bodily harm but produces temporary shock effects.

9. It usually involves just one person.

10. The travel is restricted to space and has nothing to do with time. No one returns into the past or, as far as our records go, disappears into the future.

CHAPTER III

Transported by Ecstasy

As we enter the historical centuries the records of transportation increase slowly in number and slightly in evidential value. No longer, however, do we meet with claims of translation to Heaven; the emphasis rests more on the disappearance than on the destination, as historical persons could not qualify for such exceptional religious honor.

"Eireks Saga Vidforla," an Icelandic narrative of the 14th century, is a good illustration. Eirek was the son of Thrand, King of Drontheim, and the record is that

> in the tenth year, and at break of day, as Eirek went to prayer, God's spirit caught him away, and he was never seen again in this world.*

If not a saint, Eirek was a very religious person. By his disappearance he became a preserver of the Biblical tradition of transportation regarding which, during the long centuries that followed the establishment of the Christian Church, the saints show a rather disappointing record.

Out of 14,000 saints mentioned in the Bollandists, Oliver Leroy credits only 93 women and 112 men with the feat of levitation, which yields a percentage of one over 230. The average height of levitation, "founded on serious evidence," he estimates as about 20 inches, the longest distance about 30 yards and the average duration about five minutes.** The author fails to appreciate the

*S. Baring-Gould: *Curious Myths of the Middle Ages,* London, 1869, p. 264.
**Oliver Leroy: *Levitation,* London, 1928.

difference between transportation and levitation as suggested by this single footnote:

> It is possible to account for the vanishing of the levitated person that is referred to in certain Lives (Colette of Corbie) not by the incredible height reached by the ecstatic in nis ascent, but by a phenomenon of invisibility, some instances of which are to be found in the Lives of several saints (Vincent Ferrer, Gerald Majella, Hermann Joseph of Steinfeld, Mary Raggi. (Ibid. p. 180).

In view of the spacial limits that Oliver Leroy sets to levitation, we may consider the "invisible transfers" elsewhere referred to as records of transportation.

The Italian Columba of Rieti is said to have been carried from her mother's house in Rieti to the nunnery at Spoleto 20 miles distant. The Spanish Peter Alcantara, detained at Madrid, appeared on the same day at Estramadura, a distance which could not have been covered by normal travel. St. Anthony of Padua was carried one night from Padua to Lisbon and carried back to Padua the following night so that he could defend his father accused of a crime.* St. Jean a Cruce (1542-1591) disappeared from the bed on which he languished and reappeared again some time later. St. Francis Xaverius was taken bodily from a ship on the high seas to a vessel in distress which he saved by his direction. Ammon was borne by an angel over the river Lycus. "The angels that were with Raphael took up the flagstone with Senan upon it, and bore him across the sea to a high hill in the middle of the island.**

Some of these stories are legendary, but from the literature on levitation we learn a few facts that might have a bearing on transportation also. The two outstanding

Acta Sanctorum, 13 June, Vol. XXIII, p. 201, N. 12.

**Andrew Lang of St. Senan: *The Book of Saints and Heroes,* London, 1921, p. 162

facts are that levitation, apparently, always follows upon a state of ecstasy* and that in this state the human body appears to lose considerable weight. To quote from another Catholic scholar, as carried away by his enthusiasm as were his favorite saints:

> St. Peter of Alcantara was unable to hear the lofty words of St. John, Verbum caro factum est, pronounced without falling into ecstasy and being raised above the earth. The Franciscan, Biagio of Caltanisetta, went into ecstasy simply at the name of Jesus and Mary, and, enraptured with their beauty, sprang into the air. Blessed Giles, of the Order of St. Dominick, remained suspended in the air in ecstasy for whole nights without it being possible to bring him back to earth, or even to give the least inclination to his body. After her communions, Mary of Agreda became slightly raised from the ground, like a dead body, and seemed to be so light that those who stood by were able to rock her with the slightest breath. King Philip II experienced the same phenomenon with Dr. Dominic of Jesus-Mary, who also performed the same ecstatic flights in the monastery of Valencia. St. Thomas of Villanova, whilst preaching one day in his cathedral, suddenly went into ecstasy and remained suspended in the air for twelve hours, and so on.**

Oliver Leroy, more critical than Farges, admits:

> Upon one occasion Joseph of Copertino, having recovered his senses on the top of a tree, could not come down again – a ladder had to be brought; Mother duBourg sank abruptly on her praying desk; Mary of Jesus Crucified, awakened from ecstasy, could hardly climb down the lime tree on top of which she was standing.***

Of Joseph of Copertino (1603-1663) about 100 levitations are recorded indoors and outdoors.**** The evi-

*Nothing less than *spiritual matrimony* can elevate the body, according to Joseph Lopez Ezquerra, a Spanish divine of 1690, whose work, *Lucerna Mystica pro Directoribus Animarum,* is probably the first book on levitation.

**Msgr. Albert Farges: *Mystical Phenomena,* London, 1926, p. 537

****Levitation,* p. 183.

*****Acta Sanctorum,* Vol., V, 1866.

dence was gathered two years after his death from contemporary witnesses. The same power of levitation is reported to have been shared by Dominic of Jesus-Mary.

The story of Marie d'Agreda, Superior of the Convent of the Immaculate Conception in Spain (died in 1665), is a remarkable one. Her unconscious need evidently was to save the souls of the heathen from damnation. According to M. Hello's biography, while

> she was one day praying for the savages in New Mexico, our Lord gave her to see them and bade her instruct them. In one of her ecstasies she found herself among the Indians and gave them rosaries which she had in her room, and which could not be found afterwards. She made five hundred visits. Whether "she was transported in the body she could not tell." But she managed to fulfill her mission and when the missionary who was sent out to Mexico met the Indians, he found that the Indians were already instructed and, as they said, by a woman who had been among them frequently. The statement was so surprising that Father Alonso de Benarides made a special visit to Spain, and was sent by Father Bernadin of Sienna, General of the Order of Agreda, where he met Marie, who recognized him as having seen him with other monks in America. She mentioned the day, the hour, the place, where she had seen them, and she spoke of Mexico like a person who had long lived in it.*

It is interesting to note the strenuous attempt of Catholic writers to set up differences between ecstasy and mediumistic trance. Oliver Leroy admits an alienation of the senses. He records that Elizabeth of Hungary and Paul of Soligno were quite exhausted after levitation, and that Adelaide of Aldelhausen and Dominic of Jesus-Mary vomited blood. He adds, however, "these symptoms are not interesting from our point of view because they cannot be ascribed with certainty to levitation itself.

*Alonso de Benarides: *Revised Memorial of 1634.* University of New

The same holds true of the loud cries uttered by Joseph of Copertino, which are also to be met with in the lives of Peter of Alcantara, Francis of St. Nicholas, Gerard Majella, etc."

Occasionally luminous phenomena have been recorded in levitation as in transportation. The body of Blessed Bernardino of Realino, according to Tobias de Ponte, emitted such bright rays that the room was lighted up like a smithy. The face and chest of D.D. Home, the medium, was covered sometimes with a silvery light. Dr. Fere observed two neurotics, the head and feet of whom were "radiant with an orange light during their trance."*

Nevertheless, Leroy concludes:

> Traditional Catholic theology does not admit a natural cause for levitation – though this attitude has no necessary relationship with its dogma. It regards it as a divine marvel or a diabolic trickery. The levitation of demoniacs or mediums is a parody, dismal or ludicrous, of the charisma of the saints. As to that of non-Catholic or even pagan mystics, it does not a priori deny its divine origin; the nature of the phenomenon in each case is to be judged after the moral context of the life in which it occurs.**

No room is left in this statement for primitive mystics to enter through the narrow Gate of Heaven. This need not be wondered at as in savage practices the spirits of the dead are considered to be responsible for levitation or transportation phenomena. We shall deal with this agency later. Here we wish only to point out the similar-

Mexico Press, Albuquerque, 1945; Herbert E. Bolton: *The Spanish Occupation of Texas, 1519-1690.* Southwestern Historical Quarterly, Vol. XVI, No. 1, July 1912; Herbert E. Bolton Editor: *Kino's Historical Memoir of Pimeria Alta,* Vol. I, The Arthur H. Clark Co., Cleveland, 1919.

**Levitation,* p. 196.
***Ibid.,* p. 251.

ity in phenomena between records concerning primitive magicians and Christian thaumaturges.

> The spirits in Victoria are called Mrarts, and are understood to be the souls of Black Fellows dead and gone, not demons unattached, the mediums, now very scarce, are Birraarks. They are consulted as to things present and future . . . .

At the end of the magic ceremony

> The medium is found entranced, either on the ground where the Mrarts have been talking, or at the top of a tree, very difficult to climb and up which there are no marks of anyone having climbed. The blacks, of course, are peculiarly skilled in detecting such marks.*

This compares very well with the record of Joseph of Copertino and Mary of Jesus Crucified. Savages, however, appear to be more practical than saints. They use the power to detect thieves. "A mongol lama . . . wished to discover certain stolen pieces of damask. His method was to sit on a bench, when he carried it, or, as was commonly believed, it carried him to the very tent of the thief.** Among the Yaos "the sorcerer occasionally makes men take hold of a stick, which, after a time, begins to move as if endowed with life, and ultimately carries them off bodily and with great speed to the house of the thief."***

Harry DeWindt in *Overland to America* records an experiment with an Indian medicine man. While he was closely watching, the medicine man disappeared from the tent and was found unconscious in another tent half a mile away.

A grimly realistic description in detail of a combination of savage magical practice and transportation is con-

*Andrew Lang: *Cocklane and Common Sense,* 1896, p. 41.
**Andrew Lang: *The Making of Religion, London,* 1900, p. 150.
****The Making of Religion,* p. 150.

tained in the autobiography of Chief Buffalo Long Lance. This is the story of medicine man White Dog's interview with the spirits:

> These interviews ended in many exciting ways, but always the final scene was accompanied by a howling wind which would start to roar across the top of the lodge as the spirits ceased talking. The big medicine tepee would rock and quiver under the strain of this wind, as it screeched through the poles at the top of the tepee and caused us to shake with fright. It was a startling climax. A chaotic medley of noise would come down to us from above – from the round opening at the top of the lodge where the tepee poles jutted out into the night air. Strange voices shrieking in weird pandemonium above the wailing of the winds; the clanking and jingling of unknown objects, and then a sudden jerk of the entire lodge, a flicker of the flames, a terrifying yell from the medicine man, and then he would disappear right in front of our eyes. But in that same instant we would hear him yelling for help. And looking up in the direction of his voice, we would see him hanging precariously by one foot at the top of the lodge, stripped as naked as the day he was born. The only thing that prevented him from falling and breaking his neck was his foot, which seemed to be caught in between the skin covering of the tepee and one of the slanting poles which supported it.
>
> "Kokenaytukishpewow! – Hurry!" he would yell frantically. And the men would rush for long poles with which to remove him from his dangerous, dangling perch at the roof of the lodge, lest he should fall and break his neck.
>
> How he got there no one knows; but he said that the spirits left him there on their way out. But the greatest puzzle to us youngsters was how he got stripped of all those stout bindings.

What were these stout bindings? The medicine man was undressed by four men, leaving only his breech cloth on his body, and then laid down on his back. His hands were placed together palm to palm and each pair of fingers was tied together with a rawhide thong which was drawn so tightly as sometimes to cause bleeding. His big toes were bound together in the same manner. Then a hide about the size of a blanket was wrapped tightly around him from head to foot and around this, at intervals of an inch, was wound a rawhide thong. Over this wrapper went still another hide wound tightly with a rawhide thong. The medicine man, who now "resembled a long brown cigar," literally was unable to move a finger.

Yet when he was placed in a standing position on the soles of his bare feet, he would gradually begin slightly to bend his knees and take short jumps. These jumps increased in length until he would be leaping around the four poles (within which there was a 12-foot area of sharp pegs at intervals of about an inch, a little square being left in the center).

Then suddenly, with a huge leap, he would hurl himself six feet over the sharp pegs right into the little clearing. Then the incantation began.*

**Long Lance,* New York, 1928.

CHAPTER IV

Kidnapped by Fairies

In mediaeval Ireland and Scotland fairies had a strong hold on human imagination. Accordingly, whoever rose up in the air or was mysteriously carried away had a perfectly acceptable explanation. He had only to claim that he accidently fell in with fairies, spied on them or for some reason inspired their enmity. Since such things were believed to happen, he succeeded in safeguarding his own reason and avoiding accusations of being in league with the Devil.

The Rev. Joseph Glanville cites a typical case of levitation attributed to fairies which does justice to the spirit of scientific inquiry by naming some of the parties concerned:

> A butler of a gentleman unnamed, who lived near Lord Orrery's seat in Ireland, fell in one day with the good people, or fairies, sitting at a feast. The fairies, therefore, endeavoured to spirit him away, as later they carried off Mr. Kirk, Minister of Aberfoyle, in 1692. Lord Orrery, most kindly, gave the butler security of his castle where the poor man was kept "under police protection" and watched, in a large room. Among the spectators were Mr. Greatrakes himself, and two bishops . . . . Late in the afternoon the butler was perceived "to rise from the ground, whereupon Mr. Greatrakes and another lusty man clapped their hands over his shoulders, one of them before and the other behind, and weighed him down with all their strength, but he was forcibly taken up from them; for a considerable time he was carried in the air to and fro over their heads, several of the company

still running under him to prevent him receiving hurt if he should fall."*

This case shows a good deal of agreement with ecclesiastic levitations. For transportation let us quote Robert Kirk, M.A., the great authority on fairies. Writing of a man with second sight, he says:

> His neibours often perceaved this man to disappear at a certane Place, and about one Hour after to become visible, and discover himselfe near a Bow-shot from the first Place. It was in that Place where he became invisible, said he, that the Subterraneans did encounter and combate with him.**

John Aubrey gives the magic word which accomplishes the miracle. A predecessor of Lord Duffus was transported to the French King's cellar and was found there asleep with a silver cup in his hand. Brought to the king, he told the story that the day before he was walking near his house in the Shire of Murray when

> he heard the noise of a whirlwind, and of voices crying *Horse and Hattock* (this is the word which the fairies are said to use when they remove from any place) whereupon he cried *Horse and Hattock* also, and was immediately caught up and transported through the air by fairies to that place where, after he had drunk heartily, he fell asleep and before he awoke the rest of the company were gone, and had left him in the posture wherein he was found. It is said the King gave him the cup which was found in his hand, and dismissed him.

The correspondent who sent the story to Aubrey interviewed Lord Duffus and was told that

> there has been, and is such a tradition, but that he thinks it is fabulous, and this account of it His Lordship had from his father, the present Lord's Grandfather. There is yet an old silver

Sadducismus Triumphatus, 1668, p. 131.

***The Secret Commonwealth of Elves, Fauns and Fairies.* Ms. dated 1692, 1933 edition.

> cup in his Lordship's possession still, which is called the Fairy Cup, but has nothing engraven upon it except the Arms of the Family.*

Robert Kirk writes of having spoken to several women who claimed that they had been taken away to nurse fairy children in Fairy Land. From Sweden comes a remarkable account of such a case. According to a legal declaration by Peter Rahm, a Swedish clergyman and husband of a midwife, made on April 12, 1671,

> a little man, swart of face and clad in grey, begged for help for his wife in labor. Peter Rahm recognized him as a Troll, blessed his wife and begged her in God's name to go with the stranger. "She seemed to be borne along by the wind. After her task was accomplished . . . she was borne home in the same manner as she had gone."**

Glanville mentions that Robert Kirk, the chronicler of the fairies, himself was, in the end, carried away by them. Kirk died in 1692 at the age of 51. His tomb, in Sir Walter Scott's time, was to be seen in the east end of the churchyard of Aberfoyle, but his body was said to be absent. According to the story told by his successor, the Rev. Dr. Grahame, in his *Sketches of Picturesque Scenery,* Kirk was walking on a dun-shi, or fairy hill, and fell down in a swoon which was taken for death. After the ceremony of a seeming funeral

> the form of the Rev. Robert Kirk appeared to a relation, and commanded him to go to Grahame of Duchray. "Say to Duchray, who is my cousin as well as your own, that I am not dead, but a captive in Fairyland; and only one chance remains for my liberation. When the posthumous child, of which my wife has been delivered since my disappearance, shall be brought to baptism, I will appear in the room, when, if Duchray shall throw over my head the knife or dirk which he holds in

**Miscellanies,* 1721, p. 158.

**Edwin Sidney Hartland: *The Science of Fairy Tales,* London, 1891, p. 39.

> his hand, I may be restored to society; but if this is neglected, I am lost forever." True to his tryst Mr. Kirk did appear at the christening and was "visibly seen"; but Duchray was so astonished that he did not throw his dirk over the head of the appearance, and so to society Mr. Kirk has not yet been restored.*

The fairies also are said to be responsible for the vanishing of Merlin, the wizard, said to have been the son of an elf or fairy, and of King Arthur. Neither of them was to see death.

Thomas of Erceldoune, called the Rhymer, a 13th century Scottish poet, is the hero of a similar legend. His romance with the elf queen apparently is based on a poem which may have been his genuine work but, according to the most widely accepted opinion, is a translation of a French original. At any rate, the story grew into a legend, according to which Thomas encountered the fairy queen under the Eildon Tree, which stood on the easternmost of the three Eildon Hills.

> Having got him into her power, she took him down with her into Fairy Land, where he abode, as he deemed, for three days, but in reality for three years. At the end of that time the lady carries him back to the Eildon Tree and bids him farewell. He asks her for some token whereby he may say that he has been with her; and she bestows on him a prophetic tongue that cannot lie, and leaves him with a promise to meet him again on Hauntley Banks.

Here both the old ballads and the older romance desert us; but if we may trust Sir Walter Scott's report of the tradition current in the neighborhood, Thomas was under an obligation to return to Fairyland when-

*Sir Walter Scott: *Demonology and Witchcraft*, pp. 21-22.

ever he was summoned. Accordingly,

> while Thomas was making merry with his friends in the tower of Erceldoune, a person came running in, and told, with marks of fear and astonishment, that a hart and hind had left the neighborhood forest and were, composedly and slowly, parading the street of the village. The prophet instantly arose, left his habitation, and followed the wonderful animals into the forest, whence he was never seen to return.*

No supernatural lapse of time is noticed between the disappearance and reappearance of a person experiencing transportation. But things are different in Fairy Land. There universal tradition permits such a lapse. The effect is as if the transported person were shifted in space and time simultaneously. Instead of being deposited at a distance in the present, he is deposited in a future time.

How did this idea of supernatural lapse of time in Fairy Land arise? Hartland's view is that it is a penalty invented by the Church to frighten people from unhallowed contacts. My own view is that journeys into Fairy Land are fantasies of return into the maternal womb in search of Eve, the bisexual component which Adam had lost in the Garden of Eden when out of his rib God fashioned a female companion for him.**

The Fairy Mound or Fairy Ring is an excellent symbol for the pregnant uterus. He who is transported by the diminutive creatures living in this underground kingdom is reduced to their size, which is anywhere within the size of the fetus. The enduring feasting, dancing and merry-making in which he joins also is descriptive

*Child: *Thomas of Erceldoune,* Vol. 1, p. 318, quoted in Edwin Sidney Hartland: *The Science of Fairy Tales,* pp. 203-204.

***The Search for the Beloved,* Hermitage Press, New York, pp. 276-280.

of the life of the unborn for whom everything is provided bountifully and without effort on its part.

Fairies have no power over iron. That is why Kirk's apparition requested the throwing of a knife or dirk over his head. The prohibition in the Old Testament that in erecting an altar of stone to Jehovah no iron tools should be employed upon it (a prohibition which was observed in the building of King Solomon's Temple) originated, in my view, in an unconscious symbolization by the altar or the temple of the maternal womb, the Holy of Holies of human generation. In the silence and peace of the womb no instruments are used for the building of the human body. Hence the use of iron in fairy lore breaks the prenatal spell, and the captive of the fairies automatically is restored (re-transported) to human society.

That he is unaware of the passage of time during his captivity is to be anticipated. Time does not exist in the womb. It is a postnatal concept. The unborn, at the very best, could feel the rate of its own growth as a form of biological time. Hence, the supernatural lapse of time in Fairy Land also may be a fetal element, while the romance with the fairy queen is a fitting representation of a union with the Beloved whom we lost at that remote evolutionary period in which the separation of the sexes in the proto-human had taken place.

◄ CHAPTER V ►

Carried by the Devil

MODERN civilization may have given us many new conflicts, raising the percentage of nervous breakdown to an alarming height, but at least it has freed us of one problem: the perils of the soul, which dominated the spiritual life of mediaeval men. We no longer are surrounded and tempted by invisible demons, and our soul has no market for the Evil One. Nor do we run the risk of being accused of witchcraft and of being burned at the stake because of the occurrence of something "supernatural" that, for lack of understanding, was called the work of the devil in the past.*

In spite of the declaration by the Council of Aquileia that it was heresy to believe in the miraculous conveyance of witches through the air, theologians have argued this question back and forth for centuries. They referred to evidence that "could not be questioned," and to the confession of the majority of witches, from whom the same story kept emerging. Living in an unpsychological age, in which the existence of the unconscious and its range of powers was not even suspected, they knew nothing of the shaping power of prevailing belief over unexplainable happenings; they failed to introject that which the witches and the possessed projected. When transportation actually occurred and the victim shared

*"The black art includes persons being immediately agitated by an evil spirit, carried often violently into the air by the help of the Devil, and being able to carry away others in the air also." Defoe: *A System of Magic*, p. 219.

the popular delusion that he was on the way to the Sabbath, the work of the Devil appeared clearly demonstrated. It had not dawned on them that transportation might have nothing to do with the Devil in spite of such confessions, and that the concentration of the Church on salvation was directly responsible for the emergence of the Devil as an unconscious opposite.

All mediaeval authorities agree that the witches' ointment played an important part in transportation.

> As to the ointment with which they anoint themselves, some authors, amongst others John Baptista Porta and John Wierus, boast that they know the composition. Amongst other ingredients there are many narcotic drugs, which cause those who make use of them to fall into a profound slumber, during which they imagine that they are carried to the Sabbath up the chimney, at the top of which they find a tall black man with horns, who transports them where they wish to go, and afterwards brings them back again by the same chimney.*

According to others the recipe is much more gruesome:

> Now the following is their method of being transported. They take the unguent which, as we have said, they make at the devil's instruction from the limbs of children, particularly of those whom they have killed before baptism, and anoint with it a chair or a broomstick; whereupon they are immediately carried up into the air, either by day or by night, and either visibly or, if they wish, invisibly . . . . At times he transports the witches on animals, which are not true animals, but devils in that form; and sometimes without any exterior help they are visibly carried solely by the operation of the devil's power.**

Boguet describes the various means of transport as a white staff, a broomstick, a black horse, a black goat,

**The Phantom World,* originally published in 1751, quotation from London, 1850, edition, p. 110.

***Malleus Maleficarum,* translated with an Introduction, Bibliography and Notes by the Rev. Montague Summers, London, 1948, p. 107.

a black man, or the Devil himself like a great wind. The magic word also enters into the technicalities. Isobel Gowdie, of Aldearne, one of the most talkative of Scotch witches, deposed in 1662:

> I had a little horse, and would say, "Horse and Hattock, in the Devil's name!" and then we would fly where we would, even as straws would fly upon a high wind. We will fly like straws when we please. Wild straws and corn straws will be horses to us, and we put them betwixt our feet and say, "Horse and Hattock, in the Devil's name." When we would ride we take windle straws or bean straws and put them betwixt our feet, and say thrice:
>
> *Horse and Hattock, horse and go*
> *Horse and pellatis, ho, ho!*
>
> and immediately we would fly wherever we would.*

It is worth noticing that the magic word is the same as the fairies are reputed to use in their aerial journeys. The word is different in a French story but the feasting and dancing are the same as in fairy company. The story concerns a carpenter of Heiligenstein, in Alsace, who, on October 16, 1716, was found at 5 o'clock in the morning in the garret of a cooper at Bar. The man was fast asleep and the door was fastened on the inside. The story of the carpenter was that at four in the morning he set out for Bar (the distance of a quarter of an hour from Heiligenstein), when suddenly he saw,

> in a place covered with verdure and grass, a magnificent feast, brightly illuminated, where a number of persons were highly enjoying themselves with a sumptuous repast and by dancing; that two women of his acquaintance, inhabitants of Bar, having asked him to join the company, he sat down to table and partook of the good cheer, for a quarter of an hour at the most; after that, one of the guests having cried out, "Cito, cito," he found himself carried away gently to the cooper's garret. This

*Sergeant: *Witches and Warlocks,* p. 39.

> is what he declared in the presence of the magistrate. The most singular circumstance of this history is that hardly had the carpenter deposed what we read, than those two women of Bar who had invited him to join their feast hung themselves, each in her own house. The superior magistrates, fearing to carry things so far as to compromise perhaps half of the inhabitants of Bar, judged prudently that they had better not inquire further; they treated the carpenter as a visionary, and the two women who hung themselves were considered as lunatics; thus the thing was hushed up, and the matter ended.*

The Devil apparently speaks Latin in France. "Cito" means quick. Our carpenter fell in with the witches and was only transported afterwards as in typical fairy stories, but the assumption that he invented the first part of the story in order to give it a rationale is complicated by the alleged double suicide. However, the judge's attitude was so commendably sober that the story is worth mentioning.

Many less spectacular cases deserve more serious consideration. Of Florence Newton, of Youghal, tried at the Cork Assizes in 1661 as a witch, it was testified:

> . . . the Maid was removed strangely, in the Twinkling of an Eye, out of Bed, sometimes into the Bottom of a Chest with Linnen, and the Linnen not at all disordered; sometimes betwixt the two Beds she lay on; sometimes under a Parcell of Wooll; sometimes betwixt his bed and the Mat of it in another room; and, once, she was laid on a small Deal Board which lay on top of an House between two Solar Beams, where he was forc'd to rear up ladders to have her fetch'd down.**

In the days of Salem witchcraft, Sarah Good, who was under the guard of three men at Constable Baybrook's house, during the night "was gone SOME TIME

*Calmet: *The Phantom World,* p. 135.
**John Ashton: *The Devil in Britain and in America,* London, 1896, p. 266.

FROM them, both barefoot and barelegged. That same night, Elizabeth Hubbard, one of the afflicted persons, complained that Sarah Good came and afflicted her, being barefoot and barelegged, and Samuel Silby (who was courting Elizabeth Hubbard), struck her on the arm." Allen Putnam, in telling this story,* pertinently asks that if she disappeared how did Michael Dunnell and Jonathon Baker, the two assistant guards, know that she was barefoot and barelegged? He says that "they perhaps saw her stockings and shoes when she was not to be seen."

Several reports of a similar nature appear in Cotton Mather's *The Wonders of the Invisible World,* edition of 1862.

At the trial of Bridget Bishop at Salem on June 2, 1692, the following is reported from William Stacey's testimony:

> This deponent having been threatened by Bishop, as he was in a dark Night going to the Barn, he was very suddenly taken or lifted from the Ground, and thrown against a Stone-wall: After that, he was again hoisted up and thrown down a Bank, at the end of his House. (p. 137.)

> In the trial of Susanna Martin on June 29, 1692, Joseph Ring testified that he "has been strangely carried about by Demons, from one witch-meeting to another, for near two years together; and for one quarter of this time they have made him, and keep him Dumb, tho' he is now again able to speak." He was visited by unknown shapes which "would force him away with them, unto unknown Places, where he saw Meetings, Feastings, Dancings; and after his return, wherein they hurried him along through the Air, he gave Demonstrations to the Neighbors, that he had indeed been so transported. (p. 147-8.)

* *Witchcraft of New England Explained by Modern Spiritualism,* Boston, 1888, p. 324.

> In the case of Martha Carrier, tried on August 2, 1692, "One Foster, who confessed her own share in the witchcraft for which the Prisoner stood indicted, affirm'd, that she had seen the prisoner at some of their witch-meetings, and that it was this Carrier, who perswaded her to be a witch. She confessed that the Devil carry'd them on a pole to a witch-meeting; but the pole broke, and she hanging about Carrier's neck, they both fell down, and she then received an hurt by the Fall, whereof she was not at this very time recovered." (p. 158.)

Here is a paragraph from Aubrey about the risks attendant upon transportation:

> A gentleman of my acquaintance, Mr. M., was in Portugal, Anno 1655, when one was burned by the Inquisition for being brought thither from Goa in East India, in the air, in an incredibly short time.*

The translated Soldade of Antonio de Morga** narrowly escaped the same fate in Mexico City. The story first was recorded by the Friar Gasper de San Augustin in the *Conquista de las Islas Filipinas,* published in Spain in 1698. The date of the event was October 25, 1593, the place the Plaza Mayor in front of the palace. In bright sunshine a strange soldier appeared suddenly among the sentries on guard. He was dressed in the uniform of the guard of the Governor's Palace, the capital of the Filipinas. He looked dazed and stared around him like a man lost. He answered readily when challenged:

> My name is Gil Perez. As to standing sentry here, I am doing as nearly as possible what I was ordered to do. I was ordered this morning to mount guard at the doors of the Governor's Palace in Manila. I know very well that this is not the Governor's Palace, and evidently I am not in Manila. Why or how that may be, I know not. But here I am,

**Miscellanies,* p. 164.
***Five Minute Classics,* New York, 1945, p. 225.

> and this is a palace of some kind, so I am doing my duty as nearly as possible.

Then simply as if passing out a bit of gossip, the soldier remarked:

> Last night the Governor of the Filipinas, His Excellency Don Gomez Perez Dasmarinas, had his head cracked with an ax in the Moluccas and is dead of it.

When the soldier was told that he was at that moment in the City of Mexico, thousands of miles away from Manila, he would not believe it. He was examined by the viceroy and his council, who scented the Devil behind the affair and handed him over to the Holy Office. He was jailed but no examination could shake his testimony.

Two months later a galleon arrived from the Filipinas and not only brought confirmation of the governor's death the day before Gil Perez's appearance in Mexico but also had aboard it a passenger who at once recognized Gil Perez as a soldier of the Palace Guard and testified to having seen him the day before his transportation to Mexico.

The Holy Office considered him an innocent victim of the Devil and refused to convict him. Gil Perez was shipped back to the Philippines.

It is heartening to know that even though he was not transported by the Devil, Gil Perez had the Devil's luck.

◂ CHAPTER VI ▸

Borne by the Poltergeist

If we could divest the Devil from theological connotations and use the word impersonally and collectively, it would be as good and as bad a term as the Spirit of the Lord to explain mysterious disappearances and re-appearances. The logical procedure is to discuss singly all the dynamic components which appear synthetized in these two terms. Thus we come to people who speak no longer of being wafted away by angels, of travelling by magic, of being kidnapped by fairies or by his Satanic majesty, but are carried away by the Poltergeist or his kith and kin.

The word "Poltergeist" comes from the German *polter* (noise) and *geist* (ghost). It means a noisy or racketing "spirit" that hurls crockery and makes things appear and disappear. The poltergeist manifestation is an explosive energy discharge by a mischievous and often malevolent intelligence. It acts as if a secondary, hostile part of a personality had broken loose from the main stream and had established itself extraneously in space. Yet it remains closely bound to its unwilling victim whom it follows like a familiar in witchcraft stories.*

Sometimes, however, it is difficult to draw the line between the Poltergeist and the ordinary ghost. The main difference is that the Poltergeist always is attached to a person and carries on in daylight, whereas the ghost

*Hereward Carrington and Nandor Fodor: *Historic Poltergeists,* London, 1935; Nandor Fodor: *The Psychoanalytic Approach to the Problems of*

usually is attached to a house and goes bump in the night. In old accounts we find the devil or the fairies in the center of this picture; in modern ones the ghost turns into the spirit of the dead. At this point we land in a spiritualistic circle and have to determine how much of the manifestation is due to the spirit of the dead and how much to the spirit of the living. The latter borders on problems of the unconscious in every respect, the former in a good many.

In the chapter "Transportation by Invisible Power" of John Aubrey's *Miscellanies,* Poltergeist disturbances centering around a 21-year-old servant named Francis Fry are reported by the Rev. Andrew Paschal, B. D., Rector of Chedzoy, in Somerset, in a letter dated May 3, 1683:

> But the most remarkable at all happened in that Day that I passed by the Door in my return hither, which was Easter-eve when Fry returning from work (that little he could do) he was caught by the Woman Spectre by the Skirts of His Doublet, and carried into the Air; he was quickly missed by His Master and the workmen, and quite an enquiry was made for Fran. Fry, but no hearing of him; but about half an Hour after Fry was heard Whistling and Singing in a kind of Quagmire. He was now affected as he was wont to be in his Fits, so that none regarded what he said; but coming to himself an Hour after, he solemnly protested, That the Woman carried him so high that he saw his Master's house underneath him no bigger than a haycock, that he was in perfect Sense, and Prayed God not to suffer the Devil to destroy him; that he was suddenly set down in that Quagmire. The Workmen found one Shoe on one side of the House and the other Shoe on the other side; his Perriwig was espied next Morning hanging on the top of a tall Tree. It was soon observed, that Fry's

Occultism, Journal of Clinical Psychopathology, July 1945; and *The Poltergeist Psychoanalyzed,* Psychiatric Quarterly, April 1948. Both reprinted in *Haunted People,* by Carrington and Fodor, E. P. Dutton, New York, 1951.

> Part of his Body that had laid in the Mud, was much benumbed, and therefore the next Saturday, which was the eve of Low-Sunday, they carried him to Crediton to let blood; which being done, and the Company having left him for a little while, returning they found him in a Fit, with his forehead all bruised and swollen to a great Bigness, 'till he recovered himself, and then told them, that a Bird flew in at the Window with a great Force, and with a Stone in its Mouth flew directly against his Forehead. The People looked for it, and found on the ground just under where he sat. not a Stone, but a Weight of Brass and Copper, which the People were breaking and parting it it among Themselves. (P. 153.)

It is not unusual for the victim of the Poltergeist to suffer minor injuries. On the other hand, it is less common to see the Poltergeist personified, particularly by the opposite sex, as is Fry's "Woman Spectre." Let us set the Fry account against the case of Vilma Molnar, a 14-year-old Hungarian peasant girl of whom Baron von Schrenck-Notzing reports:*

> Returning home with Vilma Molnar, the lady of the house found her six-months-old child, who was left in the cradle, in the middle of the floor sitting on a cushion. Next day, the same thing happened again. The lady of the house ran out to find the servant girl. They returned together, and found the child on the floor again, covered with four cushions, happy and satisfied as if she had found a wonderful playmate. The same day a one-year-old neighbor child of whom she was taking care, twice disappeared from the lady's side. First she found her in a stall in the stable, then in the barn in a high grain basket. Vilma's clothes were scattered all over the floor of her room.

The actual arrival of a transported boy has been reported in *Psychic Research,* March 1930, by Harry Price and Miss H. Kohn, a lecturer in languages at Deccan Col-

*In *Gesammelte Aufsatze zur Parapsychologie,* Stuttgart, 1929, p. 390

lege, Poonah, Bombay University. A 9-year-old Indian boy, named Damodar Ketkar was the subject of violent Poltergeist persecution. He was levitated and suffered from complete physical exhaustion after the experience. His older brother, Ramkrishna Bapat, suddenly materialized in front of Miss Kohn's doorway like a rubber ball. He looked bright but amazed, and said, "I have just come from Karjat."

Miss Kohn's sister, who reports the event, describes the posture of the boy as most remarkable. He was bending forward when he appeared. Both his arms were hanging away from his sides, the hands limp. His feet were not touching the floor, as she saw a distinct space between them and the threshold. "It was precisely the posture of a person who has been gripped around the waist and carried, and therefore makes no effort but is gently dropped at his destination."

Today such a happening is ascribed to the Poltergeist. The feat was the same when, in witch hunting times, it was ascribed to the Devil.

> Vincent of Beauvais (Spec. Hist. XXVI, 43) relates a story told by S. Peter Damian of a five-year-old son of a nobleman, who was for the time living in a monastery; and one night he was carried out of the monastery into a locked mill, where he was found in the morning. And when he was questioned, he said that he had been carried by some men to a great feast and bidden to eat; and afterwards he was put into the mill through the roof.*

If a libidinal element entered into the situation, it was the demon lover, the incubus:

Describing the temptations of Hieronyma, in the City of Padua by an incubus, Father Sinistrari of Ameno, who

**Malleus Maleficarum*, by Rev. Montague Summers, London, 1948, p. 105.

was lecturer on Sacred Theology in the same town 25 years afterwards, says that

> Sometimes, while she was nursing her little girl, he would snatch the child away from her on her breast and lay it upon the roof, on the edge of the gutter, or hide it but without ever harming it.*

In a haunted house, it is the ghost.

In his *Haunted Houses,* Chapter VII, entitled "The fantastic Villa of Comeada, Coimbra (Portugal)," Camille Flammarion quotes Mr. Homem Christo's adventures, as told by himself in *Le Parc du Mystere,* 1923. Mr. Homem Christo rented the villa in October, 1919. He was a first-year law student expelled from the university for refusing to conform to a religious custom and for armed revolt. He moved into the villa with his young wife, his six-weeks-old-baby and two maids.

From the first day his wife complained of hearing strange noises in the house. But Mr. Christo believed that after the row at the university some practical jokers wanted to exasperate him.

After inspecting the house from cellar to attic and looking in the servants' quarters he installed himself in the suspected room.

> My wife, trembling in all her limbs, though my friend's adventure was unknown to her, put the baby's cradle at the foot of her bed upstairs, taking every precaution for the watching of the cradle and of her bolted door. She knew that she could expect no concession from me to the 'supernatural', and that the trickster or tricksters, if caught, would be brutally done to death. It was, in fact, war.

The phenomena began by the opening of the closed and bolted shutters. According to Mr. Christo, "They were both resistant and elastic to the touch, as if held

**Demoniality* or *Incubi and Succubi,* Paris, 1879, p. 43.

by muscles working against my own." He let go, bounded to the door or the passage leading into the garden. It opened suddenly. There was no human being behind the wooden shutters. He ran around the house. When he came back, the shutter closed itself. He had to call his wife to be let in. He went to get his revolver and accompanied his wife upstairs.

> As we were going up the stairs, pressed against each other, I suddenly felt her getting heavy and pulling me back with the weight of two bodies. She started crying and struggling: 'Frances, help! Somebody has got hold of my feet.'
>
> We had arrived on the small landing lighted by a window towards the garden at the back of the house.
>
> Without turning round – so convinced was I that I should not see anybody – I passed my right hand over my left shoulder and fired in that direction. The shot rang out fearfully in that sonorous house, and my wife, leaning across my arm, seemed to be dead; but I had not killed the vile thing that pursued me, for I received a violent blow on the cheek as if with five small sticks.
>
> Singularly enough, the blow on the cheek gave me back all my energy. Being struck means that one strikes out and reacts immediately. I bore my wife from the terrible grip which sought to take her away from me, and by the vague light of the window I saw once more that there was nobody behind her. We reached our room and I banged the door feverishly as if I were crushing something in the doorway. My wife, feeling herself saved, and thinking of a malefactor because I defended myself with a revolver, rushed to the cradle of her child; the cradle was empty. Then she fainted away.
>
> Savagely watching the circle of feeble light which the lamp shed around me and the woman on the floor for a sign of something which would no doubt appear there, I waited. It was useless to think of defence. Knife, revolver, all this became powerless against an enemy who could not be seized.
>
> From afar the servants, having heard the firing, howled like dogs at the moon. I know of nothing

> more demoralizing than the cries of women in the night. But the soft wailing of a baby which seemed to come from under the floor awoke me from my moral feebleness. It had to be found, the little mite, for I knew from my wife's fainting fit that it was not she who had put it away.
>
> So I had the courage – it required some courage to go up and down stairs in that house – to search the whole ground floor, holding the lamp on high. I found the infant, quite naked, all its swaddling clothes taken off, placed on its back in the middle of a marble table like an object of no value abandoned by the redoubtable robber in his haste to escape in the night.
>
> All night long I had to soothe the hysterics of my wife and the tears of my infant child. It was only at sunrise that everything returned to its natural order, and the mother went to sleep with the baby's lips on her breast.
>
> I must say that this horrible adventure put me into such a state of breakdown that I could no longer face my invisible enemy or enemies. This last conjuring trick, this baby taken from one story to another without our being able to guess how it passed the staircase – or the walls – it could not be explained, could not be tolerated.

Homem Christo's book was published in collaboration with Mme. Rachilde of whom Flammarion writes: "I have had the honour and pleasure of knowing the latter for thirty years, and know that she will not admit the reality of psychic phenomena at any price, for the respectable but disputable reason that her parents were victims of mediums."

Mrs. F. E. Leaning, a prominent member of the London Society for Psychical Research, comments* and continues:

> This seemed to me, in spite of its credentials, a wild tale at first reading, until recently I came across an account of a haunted house, not in Portugal but in the West End of London, and given, not

**Light*, April 4, 1925.

by a foreign law student, but an English doctor who uses the pseudonym of MacDonald on account of his Scottish blood, and who is known to Mr. Ralph Shirley as a perfect reliable witness. He lived next door to a family named Thompson who were subjected to the utmost inconvenience by the disappearance of keys in particular, but of other objects as well, such as a hearth brush. These things would either be found elsewhere (as in Mr. Morell Theobald's case) or would come into sight under the eyes of someone present. The hearth brush, for instance, reappeared in a horizontal position and so came down slowly to the ground, in a manner reminding us of Poltergeist works. It was hot to the touch; so were two clean collars of Mr. Thompson's though there was neither fire nor hot flat-irons in the house at the time. Miss M. L. Lewes, the authoress of *Stranger than Fiction,* in relating the haunting of an old Welsh mansion, speaks of exactly the same sort of thing.

All in the house were often annoyed by the tricks of the family ghost. Frequently books, garments, umbrellas, anything in fact, if left lying about, would disappear in the most unaccountable way. But if no notice were taken the articles were always returned in a short time.

A baby also figures in this story. A visitor had missed her infant daughter from the cradle and, after a fruitless and distracted search, was told to wait patiently and to try to sleep. As the night passed in wakeful anxiety, she had a sudden impulse to get up and look into the cradle. There lay the little one, sleeping peacefully and none the worse for its strange adventure.

Further details on the MacDonald story are given by Inkster Gilbertson, F. J. I.,* giving the date as July, 1893:

So sensitive did the maid Bridget become to the influences about the house that she was in a state of trance every day – frequently all day. Sometimes she would disappear mysteriously, and after being absent for hours, would return as mysteriously as

Occult Review, Vol. VI, pp 330-31

she disappeared. This became so troublesome that at last her mistress had to send her away. She could not keep her, so a situation was found for her in a school near Bristol.

A few days after she had gone – as recorded by Mrs. MacDonald – on March 20, 1895, "the most appalling thing happened." At seven o'clock in the evening, the Thompsons were assembled in the kitchen, for they were now without a maid, when the door burst suddenly open, and in tumbled Bridget helplessly on the floor. She was without hat or jacket or boots, and wore her ordinary house shoes – which bore no trace of travel – and a rough apron, as if she had been at work.

She was in a state of trance and remained in that condition until 11 o'clock, when on being questioned she said she had been to a friend. She seemed to remember nothing of her new place, and when asked where she went on being put into the train by Kate and Jimmy on Saturday, she replied "We don't go to Fairyland by train." She persisted in saying she had been to Fairyland since Saturday.

Mrs. Thompson, however, related that she afterwards wrote to the girl's mistress to ascertain if she had been to her new place, and received a reply to the effect that she had been there alright, but had suddenly disappeared and that she had been last seen downstairs, at work, cleaning the boy's boots.

The doctor who was present on the occasion of the girl's reappearance, before returning home that evening, went to the landing and calling upstairs said "Since you have brought back the girl, can you not send us the girl's boots, for we must send her back again?"

Almost immediately the boots were thrown down from the upper regions. He then asked for the hat and jacket in the same way. They were also sent down, the jacket falling on Mrs. MacDonald's head. The hat, which fell on the floor, was observed to be a new one, which no one in the house had ever seen before. The girl declared it was not hers, and that she knew nothing about it.

For a variation in ghostly fare let us now turn to a

story about a disused burial ground in the Canara jungle, as printed in the *Occult Review*.

Under the title "Asleep Among the Dead" Flora M. Fox tells the following story as told to her by her brother, C. P. Fox, C. E.

"I was on construction work on the Southern Mahratta railway. Rather late one evening, I arrived near Castle Rock in the Canara jungle. I had left my inspection carriage at Londa, the point where the line had been completed, and had been busy levelling for the continuation of the permanent way to Castle Rock.

"Besides my usual staff of trolley men, chain holders, and the like, I had with me my old and faithful 'boy', and my Mohammedan bearer, Nabi. As there were quantities of big game close at hand – to wit, bison, bear, panther and tiger, besides black buck and other deer – I had my shooting kit with me and had so far been lucky with my bag. Not far from Castle Rock was the dak bungalow where I proposed passing the night.

"It was a dark, misty evening, and even when the moon rose it only created a sort of pale twilight, very different from the usual brightness of an Indian night. The bungalow was, like most daks, not of an inviting appearance. On entering, I found my servants had arranged things as best they could, and dinner, apparently produced from nowhere, was ready. Having dined. I stretched myself on my long chair on the verandah with a 'butty', and buried myself in the latest novel from home.

Time went by but I was loath to turn in, as the sleeping apartment was stuffy and not too clean. So I directed my servants to bring my camp-bed outside on the verandah, which they did: and here I lay down in the soft night air, and was soon asleep. I had noticed, on my arrival, an old disused burial ground near the bungalow, with great tombs rising eerily in the mist, but had not given it much thought as a possible lurking place for game. So I had my trusty heavy-bore beside me as I slept. I slept but "with one eye open", as befitted at the time and place. My slumbers were light. Imagine, then, my amazement when I suddenly found myself broad awake – not on the verandah, but out in the old burial ground, my bedstead wedged in between two crumbling tombs.

"I was up in a moment, and of course in an unreasoning fury. To shout for the servants to threaten them with pains of death for daring to play this joke on me, was the work of an instant.

"I found them sound asleep, and when they saw the position of my bed, they trembled as with an ague, protesting with every solemn oath that they had had no hand in the matter. My bed was delivered with some difficulty – so firmly was it wedged – and moved back to the verandah. I was resolved to have no more tricks. So I lay awake, holding my rifle at my side.

"Yet I must have dozed off, for I was aroused by a strange movement and an increased blowing of the damp night air on my forehead. The swaying ceased, I was again broad awake, and again, to my amazement, in the company of the dead. I am not a nervous man, yet I must confess to a decided shock when I saw those crumbling tombs once more. How did I get there? Who moved my bed? The servants, I knew, were guiltless, for I had awoken before they had time to run away, and the terror, in the first instance, I could see was no fake. I determined, nevertheless, to remain where I was, and not to give any nocturnal spirits the trouble of moving my couch again. The tombs protected me from any draft, and I slept peacefully, having settled to myself to make the move before anyone was astir.

"I woke at daybreak – to find myself back on the verandah! Was the second incident a dream? I tried to think that it was – tried, in fact, to explain away the whole occurrence, but in vain. There, conclusive evidence, were fragments of gravelly moss clinging to the sides of my bedstead. Cumbered as I was with my rifle (which was always in my grasp) I could not possibly have moved the bed myself in my sleep. So that way out had to be dismissed.

"India is not only a 'land of regrets', also a land of mystery. I could not help thinking of a story of Kipling's in which he asks whether the gods of the East exercise power over us at times when we invade their country. Be that as it may, I never solved the mystery. The proper sequel, of course, would have been some terrible calamity either to myself or to some of my men; but nothing occurred beyond a slight superstitious uneasiness on the part of the servants, which soon passed.

"I had a successful end to my construction work on that part of the line, brought down plenty of big game and escaped fever."

The story of Angelica Darocca, the blood-sweating girl at Radein in Tyrol, belongs to modern religious phenomenology. This is how Dr. Franz Hartmann reports it.*

> The girl was desirous of leaving the place, as she felt she was a burden to her brothers, and the bishop of Trient at last got her a place in a convent at Mern. On November 17, two nuns of that convent came to take her in charge. They talked and prayed with her, and while they spoke the girl fell into a trance. When the nuns called again the next morning, they found the bed empty; the girl had disappeared and her brothers informed them that this was not the first time she had thus

Occult Review, July, 1906, Vol. IV.

> mysteriously been taken away. The parson was called, they searched the house, but Angelica was nowhere.
>
> On November 25, the brothers and some of the neighbours held their usual prayer meeting in that room, when suddenly the girl was in the same bed again. She said that some superior power had taken her away, without any volition on her part. She also did not know where she had been; but a day or two after a lady in the vicinity received a letter from a friend of hers living at Rome; in that letter she said that she and her sister had enjoyed the visit of an amiable Tyrolese girl by the name of Angelica Darocca – that she stayed with them and went with them to the Church of St. Peter; that the girl had disappeared without even taking a drink of water during that stay.

Dr. Hartmann then tells the story of Dr. Z., a friend with strong psychic faculties who was transported from Livorno to Florence, a distance of 100 kilometers, in 15 minutes:

"I had to go to Livorno for a few days. I had already been at Livorno for two days when a strange thing happened to me. It was after 9 p.m., and I had not yet dined, when I distinctly felt an occult message coming from my friends M. at Florence, asking me to come as soon as possible, because they needed my presence. Instinctively I took my cloak and, without even changing my jacket, bestrode my bicycle and went to the station, intending to take the first train leaving for Florence; but as I went on I was forced by an irresistible impulse to take the right road which leads towards Pisa, and at this same time my bicycle went on with such a velocity that I became giddy and my legs could not follow any more the quick movement of the pedals, so I had to abandon them. Still the velocity grew to such an extent that it seemed to me as if I was flying without touching the ground. For a moment I saw Pisa and its lights, then my breath began to fail me owing to the pressure of the air caused by the rapidity of the motion, and I lost consciousness.

"When I regained my senses, I found myself in the parlor of our friends M. at Florence, and they expressed their surprise, seeing that I had come so soon, as there were no trains arriving from Livorno at that hour. I looked at my watch. It was 9.30 p.m. Thus it could not have taken me more than a quarter of an hour to travel the 100 kilometers (63 miles) from Livorno to Florence, considering the time necessary to put on my cloak and get my bicycle.

"I asked our friends how I happened to enter the house, the doors being always closed at that hour, and they told me that 'Tom' (a certain spirit who frequently manifested himself in their house and used to give directions) told them to go to a certain room, called the 'magic chamber', to make certain signs and pronounce certain words. This they did and immediately there began a racket and noise as if a bomb had exploded at the window towards the street, and they heard a thump as if a human body had fallen upon the chair. They struck a light and found that the human body was myself and that I seemed to sleep. While this conversation took place, the doorbell rang violently. It was the night watchman, who claimed to have seen somebody, presumably a robber, enter the house through the window. Evidently, it was I whom he saw. Our friends told him that everything was all right and the watchman retired, apparently not quite satisfied and not fully convinced.

"While our friends went to open the door to speak with the watchman, they found a bicycle in the entrance hall. Thus it seems that my bicycle was carried through the closed door and I through the window, which was also closed. This happened in March, 1902."

"Another time," Dr. Hartmann continues, "the same gentleman while sitting in the parlour of our friends at Florence, fell into a trance, and while in this condition was taken bodily through the solid ceiling of the room above. I myself repeatedly have seen materialized ghosts which were apparently perfectly solid, pass in this way through floors and walls; but Dr. Z. was not a ghost.

"At one time the family of M. found Dr. Z. on the sofa in their parlour, after he had made an aerial trip, in a semi-conscious condition and not fully materialized. They lifted his limbs which seemed as light as a feather. He spoke to them in a whisper and asked to be magnetized, which they did. After a few minutes his strength and solidity returned, and as he jumped up and struck with his fist upon the table, he exclaimed with his usual voice, 'now I am material again'."

Dr. Hartmann is an occultist who does not believe in spirits. While noting that an intelligence called Tom seemed to have something to do with things that happened to Dr. Z., he expressed the opinion that

> these beings could not be any disembodied human spirits; for it is not reasonable to suppose that the human soul or astral form should by dying acquire such powers, and living people temporarily abandoning their physical forms do not possess them.

There is no reason why transportation should be a human monopoly once an extraneous agency appears to be involved. Here is a typical story about the transportation of a cow:

At Birchen Bower, Hollinwood, England, the mummified body of Miss Beswick, preserved under the terms of an ancient will at the Manchester Natural History Society (until 1869) was exhibited every 21 years.

> In the morning . . . when the corpse was fetched the horses and cows were always found let loose, and sometimes a cow would be found up in the hay-loft, although how it came there was, indeed, a mystery, as there was no passage large enough to admit a beast of such magnitude. The last prank of this description played by Miss Beswick, so far as our information goes, was a few years ago, when a cow belonging to the farmer then tenanting the place was found on the hay-loft, and it was the firm belief of many thereabouts that supernatural agency had been employed to place it there . . . . How the cow got up was a mystery to everyone, while that blocks had to be borrowed from Bower Mill to let it down through the hay-hole outside the barn was an equally well known fact.*

In a stone throwing case reported in the Colombo *Observer,* October, 15, 1863, it was said: "The dogs often ran howling out of the house, and were shortly afterwards found on the roof without any possibility of getting up thither of their own accord."**

Here is a quotation from the London *Daily Mail,* May 18, 1906, about a horse: "Barrels of lime were hurled downstairs, with no one near them. A horse vanished from the barn and was found in the hay room. A partition had to be knocked down to get him out."

At Prignano, Italy, in 1936, a pair of oxen took the strange trip:

> Phenomena of incendiary infestation have been recently established on a farm in Prignano (Salerno): fires broke out spontaneously, destroyed household objects, and burnt persons and animals. Bricks and stones fell in the rooms, although the windows were closed. There was spontaneous displacement of objects. A pair of oxen were even found to have been carried from one stall to another without human agency. The carabinieri, assisted by young fascists and other local persons after long and careful

*John H. Graham: *The Haunted Homes and Family Traditions of Great Britain,* London, 1905, p 348.

***Spiritual* Magazine, 1865, p. 66.

> observation came to the conclusion that it was impossible for anyone to play a bad joke. An anonymous Neapolitan doctor and psychical researcher who was on the spot found a 16 year old girl with strong mediumistic faculties who was the involuntary means of the striking phenomena.*

Having concentrated on its transportation activities, we have left a great deal unsaid about the Poltergeist. But enough has been stated to reveal it as a dangerous madcap. Nor is his cousin, the common ghost, a pleasant bedfellow. How do they do it? That is a problem to which we still have no answer.

**Ali del Pensiero,* April, 1936, p. 448.

◂ CHAPTER VII ▸

Conveyed by Spirits

THE Poltergeist, as we have seen, is a mischievous spirit – much like a mischievous child. Usually it is associated with children, although where it appears to be the agency in transportation children may not always be involved. However, children figure prominently in a closely similar type of transportation case where the spirits are of the seance room rather than of the crockery-throwing variety.

Even if we have brought spiritualistic "spirits" into the picture, long-range transportation which involves children and which does not take place under pre-arranged conditions, is virtually a fool-proof demonstration of psychic agency and power. To cheat distance is impossible and children do not knowingly, or willingly, place themselves in the frightening situations of the transported. Furthermore, transportation is a type of phenomenon that does not lend itself readily to exploitation by those who enjoy mischief, crave notoriety or desire to hoax.

In cases where children are surrounded by adults, how long could the air of mystery over their disappearance and reappearance elsewhere be maintained if the claim were spurious? Consider the Pansini children of Bari who succeeded in keeping the Italian press busy for several weeks with their mysterious adventures.

Here is a report from the *Giornale d'Italia,* dated Bari, November 15, 1905, and titled, "A Mysterious Residence."

"In the year 1901 Signor Maura Pansini, a mason and architect, went with his family to live in an old house not far from the Palazzo Municipale. A few days passed off quietly, but then the family was terrified by strange noises and phenomena; the pictures fell from the nails, plates, glasses and bottles were thrown against the walls and broken to pieces, and the furniture moved about without anyone touching it. They concluded that the place was haunted by evil spirits; the priest was called and went through the prescribed ceremony for exorcising the devils; but even the most liberal application of prayers and holy water availed nothing; the tables were overturned and chairs were broken just as before.

"One evening the little Alfredo Pansini, aged seven years, while the rest of the family were present, fell into a state of sleep and began to speak in a voice which was not his own, saying that he had been sent by God for the purpose of driving away the evil spirits. It seemed for a while as if a better class of spirits had come, for now there were all kinds of sweets, candy and chocolate, brought to them by the invisibles; and one night the little boy, while in a state of trance, described a battle taking place between the good and bad ghosts. Next, the boy began to walk mechanically and answer questions concerning things which he could not know. They took the boy to Church. There he became as insensible as a corpse, but woke up as the bishop called his name. He remained with the bishop for several days and then returned to his parents. There still more curious phenomena took place.

"One day the lad Alfredo, with his brother Paolo, aged eight years, were at Ruvo at 9 A.M.; and at 9:30 they were found at the Capucine Convent at Malfetta (some 30 miles away). Another day the whole family were sitting at the breakfast table at 12:00 o'clock and as there was no wine the little Paolo was sent for it. He did not return, and an hour afterwards Alfredo suddenly disappeared, and at 1 P.M. both boys were found in a fishing boat on the sea, not far from the port of Barletta. They began to cry, and the fisherman, being himself frightened almost out of his wits by their sudden appearance, took them ashore, where by good fortune they found a coachman who knew them and took them home, where after a rapid drive of half an hour they arrived at 3:30. In this way they were spirited away on other occasions to Bisceglie, Giovinnarri, Mariotti and Ferlizzi (the distance of which places from Ruvo may be seen on the map) and brought back to their parents in the ordinary way.

"The Doctor Raffaelo Estugno and other scientists investigated their cases, but they either came to no result, or they avoided giving the only reasonable explanation which presents itself to an occultist; and this is not to be wondered at, if we take into consideration the storm of indignation which has been raised in "scientific" quarters even against such a celebrated scientist as Professor Richet for publishing the accounts of his experiments in the Villa Carmen, and having had the hardihood to affirm publicly having seen and touched a materialized ghost."

It is impossible to wish for better evidence of human transportation than two boys dropping into a boat, in open sea, out of the blue. The story is unprecedented. Among the people who attested the diversified flying adventures of the Pansini boys are some important ecclesiastical functionaries, as Berardi Pasquale, Bishop of Ruvo and Bitonto, Archbishop Guilo Vaccaro di Bari, Archdeacon Vallarelli di Terlizzi, Cavalier Carmarino, magistrate Mellusi, delegate of Bari, Father Vito Garretti and the editor of the *Corriere delle Puglie.*

Dr. Joseph Lapponi, who was chief physician to Pope Leo XIII and Pius X, gives further information on this extraordinary case.* He interviewed a member of the family and makes it clearer than the *Giornale d'Italia's* account that the phenomena of the Pansini children covered a period of three years. They began with Alfredo when he was seven and his two years younger brother, Paolo, did not become a partner in the Peter Pan flying concern until three years later. He also adds the following to their adventures.

> One day the two boys were in the Piazza di Ruvo at 1.35 o'clock, and at 1.45, about ten minutes afterwards, were at Trani, before the door of the house of one of their uncles, Signor Girolamo Maggiore. Passing into an hypnotic state, and being questioned, Alfredo replied to many difficult questions, to the amazement of all. Among other things which he announced, he said that he would not be able to leave on the morrow, but only after fifteen days. The next day his uncle's horse was ill, and the aunt then hired a vehicle to take the nephews back to Ruvo. But hardly had they reached their parents than they disappeared afresh, and were again found at Trani. Being taken back to Ruvo, they disappeared yet again, and were found at Bisceglie, whence it was concluded to be useless to fight against supernatural forces, and they were reconducted to Trani to await the end of the fortnight.

Presumably, these mysterious journeys, for which a trance communicator calling himself Cavallieri Fernandez claimed responsibility, stopped as the originator, Alfredo Pansini, approached the age of puberty, as we have no further record. The case also is important by reason

***Hypnotism and Spiritism*, Longmans, Green and Co., New York, 1907, pp. 127 – 33.

of the collective aspect of transportation. It is a rare feature but we meet with it elsewhere, too, in the adventures of other Peter Pans.

T. L. Nichols, M.D., in *A Biography of the Brothers Davenport,* 1864, writes of the early youth of the two boys (Ira Erastus and William Henry), sons of a police official of Buffalo who years later made a spectacular, international stage career:

> One day by rapping and then trance speech the presence of a "George Brown" was signalled. He described himself as a Canadian farmer. He had been robbed and murdered in a place which he described by members of the notorious Townsend gang. He said he resided at Waterloo, W. C. and his family still lived there. Little faith was placed in the story, though the sheriff of the county declared that a George Brown used to live sixty miles away at Waterloo, whereupon the "ghost" announced (p. 42) that he intended to take Ira to the scene of his murder. Not much attention was paid to what was considered an absurd threat; but the boy, a few evenings after, while engaged in his daily task of delivering evening papers, first felt "queer", then lost his consciousness, and found himself standing in the snow, with no tracks around him to show how he had come there, in a solitary place, a mile and a half from home, on the right bank of the Niagara River. "George Brown", at his next visit, declared that he had carried him across the river, which is half a mile wide, and brought him back again, just as an experiment; but as the boy was unconscious all the time, until he found himself on the bank, while his family was getting alarmed at his absence, and as nobody saw him carried across the river, we have only George Brown't testimony on the subject, which we are not obliged to believe without a sufficient corroboration.

Ira was the older of the two boys, less than 14 at this time. Later the experience was duplicated with the simultaneous transportation of both boys.

"John King" advised the father of the Davenports, at an early stage, to take his two sons away from Buffalo, that it was dangerous for them to stay, and that they were needed elsewhere. Mr. Davenport would not consent either to leave his family with them or allow them to go . . . . . A strange event which took place as the result, apparently, of this conversation, is variously vouched for; but I have preferred to take the facts from the lips of Mr. Ira Davenport, the elder of the two brothers. He says that he was walking one evening, at about 9 o'clock, in the streets of Buffalo with his brother William, this being in the winter of 1853-4 and the boys in their 12th and 14th year.

Here Ira's recollection ceases. The next thing he knew was that he found himself and his brother in a snow bank, in a field, with no tracks near him, near his grandfather's house, at Mayville, Chautauqua County, New York, 60 miles from Buffalo. On waking up William, who had not returned to consciousness, they made their way to their grandfather's house, where they were received with surprise and their story heard with astonishment. Their father was immediately informed by telegraph of their safety and whereabouts, and he, good obstinate man, set himself to find out how they got to Mayville. On inquiry, he found that no railway train could have taken them, after the hour they left home, more than a portion of the distance, and the conductors on the road knew the boys and had not seen them. "John" declared through the trumpet, after their return home, that he had transported them, or caused them to be transported, simply to show Mr. Davenport that they could be taken to any distance as easily as they could be carried about the room, and to show him that it was useless for him to try to keep them in Buffalo. The boys, so far as I can judge from the manner in which the story was related to me by Ira, undoubtingly believe that they were taken by no ordinary means of conveyance, and that the difficulties of the journey were overcome in some unexplainable and inexplicable manner by the same power, whatever that may be, which has for eleven years worked in their presence so many marvels, not less difficult to explain than their trip from Buffalo to Mayville. They do not say that

> they were carried all the way, or part of the way. They think they must have walked a long distance for their feet were blistered. They were there, and knew not how. (pp. 48-52)

Appearing in a snow field without any tracks is almost as good evidence of a miraculous journey as the appearance of the Pansini brothers in a boat at sea.

The Rev. Jesse Babcock Ferguson, one of the most noted American preachers in the South before the Civil War, supported the Davenport records in these words:

> From as good testimony as I have of any fact that I can accept without personal knowledge, I believe that these young men have been raised into the air to the ceilings of rooms, and have been transported a distance of miles by the same force and intelligence, or intelligent force that has for eleven years worked in their presence so many marvels.*

While nothing was seen of the physical mechanism that accomplished transportation, the levitation of the brothers Davenport left behind telltale marks on the ceiling, and also exposed to the eye two gigantic hands and a monstrous arm that certainly did not belong to any of those present. Because of this unusual element, it is worth quoting from Nichols' book (pp. 33-35) the detailed story:

"At the seances, which now began to be held regularly, the manifestations already described were repeated. Loud raps were heard; the table answered questions; spectral forms were seen in the flash of a pistol; lights appeared in the upper parts of the room; musical instruments floated in the air, while being played upon, above the heads of the company. It would be too much to expect of human nature to suppose that all these things were witnessed with simple faith and open-mouthed credulity. There

*T. L. Nichols: *Supermundane Facts in the Life of the Rev. J. B. Ferguson*, London, 1865.

were enough to say it was a trick, and to be determined to detect it. Probably nine out of ten, when told of what occurred, declared it all a humbug, and that they could detect and expose it. Consequently, a close watch was kept upon the Davenports. Persons were appointed to hold them. The whole company took hold of hands when the room was darkened, that each might watch for the two next him. On one occasion, four persons selected for the purpose held the two boys; four others securely grappled Mr. and Mrs. Davenport; and even the little Elizabeth was held by two others. Every possible precaution was taken.

"When all this had been arranged, Ira was lifted bodily into the air, until he rose above the heads of those who held him, and floated away close to the ceiling. Then both boys, Ira and William, were laid upon the table, and Mr. Plympton, a well-known auctioneer of Buffalo, was requested to hold them firmly by the feet. He seized their ankles, when Ira was raised bodily into the air, followed by William. Not succeeding in holding both, he next tried the youngest, who, in spite of his added weight, was raised up with such force that his head broke through the ceiling of lath and plaster. Mr. Plympton had held to the boy with all his strength, but letting go, to prevent being himself drawn he knew not where, the boy, suddenly freed, went up by lunar attraction, let us say, or terrene repulsion – with the result to his skull and the plaster already stated. The people who heard the crash thought the boy was killed and called for a light; but he was found to be quite unhurt. There was no mistake, however, about the hole in the ceiling.

"Once the entire store of family crockery and glassware was invisibly taken from the shelves in the dark and piled upon the table. Then the boys were raised up and placed upon the dishes, and all the chairs heaped upon the table, without the agency of any mortal hand that could be discovered. All this was done without the fracture of a single article, and in total darkness. Lights were struck, and with great care the boys and chairs were taken down. The lights were again extinguished, and every article was restored to its proper place in the pantry, without the slightest mishap or accident."

On other occasions "the two boys were raised from their chairs, carried across the room and held up with their heads downward before a window. An eye-witness said, "We distinctly saw two gigantic hands, attached to about three-fifths of a monstrous arm; and those hands grasped the ankles of the two boys, and thus held the lads, heels up and heads downwards, before the window: now raising, now lowering them, till their heads bid fair to make acquaintance with the carpets on the floor. This curious, but assuredly not dignified exhibition was several times repeated; was plainly seen by every person present. Among these persons was an eminent physician, Dr. Blanchard, then of Buffalo, now of Chicago, Illinois, who was sitting in a chair by the side of Elizabeth Davenport; and all present saw an immense arm, attached to no apparent body – growing as it were, out of space – glide along near the floor, until it reached around Dr. Blanchard's chair, when the hand grasped the lower back round of Elizabeth's chair, raised it from the floor, with the child upon it, balanced it, and then raised it to the ceiling. The chair and child remained in the air, without contact with any person or thing, for a space of time estimated to be a minute, and then descended gradually to the place it first occupied."

We only can guess why, in these instances, the levitation of the boys should be accomplished by such an agency as a giant arm. It may be a matter of leverage but that explains very little about the non-human entity to which the arm was supposed to belong or the process by which it became visible and tangible. We quote this paragraph only in support of spiritualistic contentions that levitation or transportation is closely bound up with the agency of the spirit of the dead.

A fairly safe rule in the treatment of psychic phenomena is that when something totally new is introduced, the utmost caution should be observed. The case of 18-year-old Ophelia Corrales, the daughter of Buonaventure Corrales, a landowner of San Jose, Costa Rica, is a good illustration. She had two younger sisters, Bertha 12 and Flora 7, and a younger brother, Miguel 10. According to the account of Dr. Alberto Brenes, Professor of the Law Academy, dated March 5, 1908,* the three young children disappeared from a seance room one by one, were found in a nearby pavillion, the door of which was locked, and then were simultaneously re-transported. The children apparently had fun. No mention is made of their entrancement and their own story is just what is compatible with their range of imagination. They told of feeling a pressure under the arm, after which they were lifted up in the air and placed where they were found. As if the material barrier did not exist at all, they described an ordinary flight, the kind that all Peter Pans would relish.

In a letter to *El Siglo Espirita,* the organ of the Mexican Spiritist Federation, published on March 28, 1908, Don Rogelio Fernandez Guell, Mexican Consul at Baltimore, describes a novel kind of transportation for which we have no precedent:

**Annals of Psychic Science,* Vol. IX.

> One evening in the early part of November, 1908, we left Ophelia outside the seance room in the patio of the house and closed the door. We then asked her to project her double, which she immediately did. This double exactly reproduced the voice and appearance of Ophelia, but the costume was different. We asked the medium to transmit to the double a handkerchief and a comb which was in her hair, and the two articles were sent simultaneously although all openings were closed.
>
> Whilst the double talked with the spectators, the medium remained outside knocking at the door and continuing to speak, in order to assure us of her presence in the patio. "Come, Ophelia!" was said, and instantly she was in the midst of the spectators.

This is the type of phenomenon which a vivid imagination but lack of sufficient knowledge of the range of mediumistic power would suggest.

There is one more case of transportation for which Dr. Brenes is ready to vouch, but only on the basis of his intimate knowledge of the persons concerned:

> It happened once that Mlle. Ophelia proposed to go with her father to the town, but as she was not ready, her father set out alone, walking slowly so as to give her time to catch up to him. He reached the Square called "de la Fabrica". There, all of a sudden, he heard a deep breath, and she appeared in front of him as though she had come up out of the ground. A working woman and a young girl who were passing by were witnesses of the incident which, as can easily be understood, greatly surprised them, because they were quite unable to explain it.
>
> Ophelia stated that when she left home, as she thought her father was already some distance ahead, she mentally formulated the wish to be transported close to him, and that immediately she heard the voice of "Mary" who said, "I am going to please you. Count, one, two, three." She obeyed, and had hardly uttered the last word when she felt herself at the spot mentioned, about six

> hundred yards in a straight line from where she had been.

Some time after this "Mary" came to grief. She was playing doubles and lost; a strange girl was found to have been fraudulently introduced and photographed. The story was told by Ophelia's own father in a letter to W. T. Stead, published by the *Voz de la Verdad,* and though "Mary", contrite and repentant, was ready to submit to any new test, by 1914 Ophelia retired from the psychic stage.

◄ CHAPTER VIII ►

Falling into the Fourth Dimension

WE have reached a point at which the problem of human transportation no longer is a matter of calm contemplation of legend and folklore, but a violent assault against logical and scientific thinking. The claims to these mysterious happenings do not die as we reach the experimental age, but rather multiply and unfold more fully attested. Moreover, for the source of the power which accomplishes transportation, we have seen the spirits of the dead brought in by spiritualists.

Whether one approves of Spiritualism as a religion, psychic science or psychotherapy, the new approach has had the tremendous advantage of making transportation a near laboratory phenomenon. We find it recurring under generally the same conditions with the same dramatis personae in the presence of increasingly more numerous witnesses. But we also find, perhaps as a psychological check to a state of affairs gravely disturbing orthodox thinking, the theory that the actors in the transportation drama disappear via the fourth dimension in much the same way that a hypothetical two-dimensional object (possessing length and breadth only) would transcend the boundaries of a circle by being lifted up into the third dimension (of height) and deposited again on the two-dimensional plane outside the circle. On the two-dimensional level of existence, the object would vanish and reappear mysteriously at another point in space.

This hyper-space theory does not bar an extraneous

agency, to which the fourth dimension might be a sporting ground or native habitat, but it eliminates thinking of divine intervention, of a magical act or of the agency of the Devil or Poltergeist. On the basis of this theory, transportation might be due to a knack of fourth-dimensional functioning, haphazard, unconscious or willed, or it might be accidental due to a warp or fault in space (an idea which we meet frequently in science fiction). If persons do fall through a hole in space, we would have the advantage of being able to explain what happens to those who do not return. They may fail to find the entrance point, like a man who falls into a frozen river through a hole and is carried away by his own momentum or by the current underneath the sheet of ice.

A remarkable case in which exactly this appears to have happened is related by Stuart Palmer:*

In the afternoon of September 23, 1880, David Lang, a farmer living near Gallatin, Tenn., spoke to his wife on the porch of their home and then walked away across a 40-acre field. He was fully visible to his wife and to his two young children, who were playing near the porch. Meanwhile, August Peck, a Gallatin lawyer, and his brother-in-law were driving up in a horse-drawn buggy along the road in front of the house. Peck, who had come to see Lang on business, noticed him crossing the field while still a quarter of a mile away and drew air into his lungs to call out.

Lang was in the middle of the field, the grass of which had been cropped short by horses. There were no obstructing stones or trees. He was in full view of three pairs of adult eyes. At that precise moment he disappear-

*"How Lost Was My Father," *Fate* Magazine, July, 1953.

ed with an abruptness that made Peck think the ground had caved in under him.

The surface of the field, however, was unbroken. Peck, his brother-in-law and Lang's hysterical wife searched every inch of it. They found nothing to show where or how Lang had disappeared. Later that day neighbors also searched without result. For weeks afterward the field was crowded with the well-meaning and the curious, but no trace of Lang was found. A county surveyor said there was no possibility of a cave-in as limestone bedrock lay a few feet under the soil of the field.

A strange feature of the case is that, although Lang had vanished utterly from the familiar world, he evidently was not quite out of touch with it. The following spring his two children, George, eight years old, and Emma, 11, noticed that in the middle of the field where their father had disappeared was an irregular circle of rank grass some 15 feet in diameter. Horses avoided the grass within the circle, as did grasshoppers, ants and other insects.

On a sudden impulse as she stood at the edge of the circle, Emma called out to her father. George joined her. They called repeatedly and were about to leave when the incredible happened. Faint and far-off, they heard the voice of a man calling for help — a voice which Emma was certain was her father's. She told the experience to her mother, who said she also had heard the voice. However, the fact that it had grown fainter each day had led her to abandon any hope it might have held out.

If Lang indeed had fallen into a hole in space, and if time in his new habitat paralleled that here, he evidently managed to survive for several months. During this period he must have searched constantly for the point at which he had entered — and failed to find it.

The idea that there may be a knack of fourth-dimensional functioning was first put forward in psychical research by F. W. H. Myers in his great book, *Human Personality and its Survival of Bodily Death.* He coined a rather formidable term for it: "psychorrhagic diathesis." By it he meant a breaking loose of elements of the human psyche which have the ability of affecting space.* The idea was not appreciated at the time when it was broached. Yet it contains the germ of a momentous theory. It well may be that the phenomenon of human transportation may force upon us the hypothesis that at times, in states of trance and ecstasy, an energy is released from the unconscious which enables us to transcend the limitations of three-dimensional space.

Sir Ernest Wallis Budge, the great authority on ancient Egypt and Chaldea, formerly keeper of the mummies in the British Museum, declared in an interview given to the *Daily Express* on January 17, 1934:

> I knew an African and an Indian who could vanish into air as you spoke to them, touched them. Like the Cheshire cat in 'Alice in Wonderland', first they were there, then there was only the grin, then that, too, disappeared.
>
> It was no question of hypnotism, for I walked through the spot where they had been standing. In the same way they would reappear, and, as they solidified, push me away.

There was a hue and cry because of this interview, and Budge was forced to declare it as unauthorized. The wording that as they solidified they pushed him away

*I have discussed the significance of this as a comprehensive alternate theory for the understanding of psychic phenomena in "Inversion of Time and Space," *Light,* Dec. 25, 1931.

suggests that these persons knew how to find the same hole in space through which they disappeared.

In the now defunct Ghost Club of London I heard the story of a personal experience of the same nature by Capt. Pierce, a man of wide interests and travels. It happened in the Canadian backwoods but how was never quite clear to him. Something came over him just as he looked at his wristwatch. A moment later he was in new and strange surroundings, 100 miles from the spot where he looked at his watch. The travel of which he had no conscious knowledge was absolutely instantaneous and he felt none the worse for the experience.

Jean Durant, a 24-year-old French Canadian whose story is dated 1898, claimed control over the phenomenon, until one day he lost it and was never seen again. I take the story from an article by Ray Preedy in *Guide and Ideas,* London, November 14, 1936. According to this article, three doctors tested Durant's claim that he could disappear from a locked room and appear in the next one. A man named Williams gave a signed and sworn testimony that he actually had seen Durant fade away into nothingness, his dressing gown collapsing and falling down on the floor. But Durant became ill after his experience and put it down to being watched.*

Hence in subsequent tests by medical men and the police Durant demanded that only the door of the cell in which he was locked should be kept under observation. In these tests, Preedy says, Durant sometimes was secured with handcuffs and fastened to the cell wall with a heavy length of chain, the door being sealed at half a dozen points with wax. Yet he appeared suddenly among

*It means that being rendered self-conscious inhibits that which is purely unconscious.

the watchers. The handcuffs were on the floor, the lock on them intact and the seals on the door unbroken.

Finally Durant was invited to a demonstration in Chicago. His arms and legs were pinioned and the cell door closed and sealed. This time he failed to appear. After an hour's waiting the cell was opened. The rope and handcuffs were on the floor but Durant was gone and nobody ever saw or heard of him again.

How did Durant do it? We have a hint in the statement of a doctor who, before Durant appeared at his side, heard sounds of heavy breathing from the far side of the door. It sounded like a man in deep sleep. From this we may assume that Durant, like so many others, went into a state of trance, and what happened after that was beyond his control. As he had no misadventure before, he did not expect any, but apparently he trusted his luck too far.

That the need of self-preservation may be a motive behind transportation, appears from an interview with Mrs. Kathleen Barkel, published in *Light,* January 19, 1934, in which she speaks of a weird adventure in a crowded shopping district of West Croydon:

> While walking with a friend, I was apparently hit by a motor car. I felt a concussion. The next moment I found myself in the doorway of a shop some distance away. On recovering my senses I turned back and saw that a crowd had collected around the motor car. They were looking for a body which had mysteriously disappeared. My friend was in an agony. When I walked up to her she just gaped at me. Apparently at the moment that I was hit by the car I bounced off, unseen by anyone, like a rubber ball and experienced instantaneous transportation.

D. D. Home, the famous medium, narrates a similar incident in a letter to the editor of the *Spiritual Magazine,*

1861, p. 61. He was staying at the Chateau de Cercay, half an hour from Paris, and went hunting in the park. The game used to go for shelter to an immense poplar tree. Towards this he advanced cautiously.

> When close up to it I was raising my head to look for my game, when on my right I heard someone call out, "Here, here!" My only feeling was surprise at being thus suddenly addressed in English. Desire to have a good look out for my game overruled my curiosity as to whom the exclamation had come from; I was continuing to raise my head to the level of the hedge, when suddenly I was seized by the collar of my coat and vest and lifted off the ground; at the same instant I heard a crashing sound, and then all was quiet. I felt neither fear nor wonder. My first thought was that by some accident my gun had exploded, and that I was in the spirit land; but, looking about, I saw that I was still in the material world – there was the gun still in my hand. My attention was then drawn to what appeared to be a tree immediately before me, where no tree had been. On examination this proved to be the fallen limb of the high tree under which I was standing. I then saw that I had been drawn aside from this fallen limb a distance of six or seven feet. I ran, in my excitement, as fast as I could to the chateau . . . . The limb which had thus fallen measured sixteen yards and a half in length, and where it had broken from the trunk, it was one yard in circumference. The part of the limb which struck the very spot where I had been standing, measured 24 inches in circumference, and penetrated the earth at least a foot.

The incident, at best, is a case of levitation, a very frequent occurrence with D. D. Home, but it is worth including here as, together with Mrs. Barkel's story, it may establish self-preservation as a trigger that releases the energy with which transportation is accomplished. The same unconscious need was operative in the case of Apollonius of Tyana when he is said to have saved himself from the wrath of Emperor Domitian by disappearing.

> When the question of the fourth dimension was brought up by Prof. Zollner of Leipzig, Lazar von Hellenbach asked his medium whether a human being could disappear by way of that dimension. The answer was "a human being could, under certain conditions. There is too much respect for it to do it often, but there are cases when human beings disappeared and became invisible to the persecutors, as did Christ in the Temple."*

Hints at the dynamics of the transition into another dimension might be found in some transportation instances quoted by Charles Fort in his book, *Lo:*** "According to the *Courrier de l'Isere,* two little girls, last of December, 1842, were picking leaves from the ground, near Clavaux (Livet), France, when they saw stones falling around them. The stones fell with uncanny slowness. The children ran to their homes, and told of the phenomenon, and returned with their parents. Again stones fell, and with the same uncanny slowness. It is said that relatively to these falls the children were attractive agents. There was another phenomenon, an upward current, into which the children were dragged, as if into a vortex. We might have had data of mysterious disappearances of children, but the parents, who were unaffected by the current, pulled them back." (p. 27)

Instead of a vortex we find the victims dragged downwards into a hole in the following instance:

"Early in the morning of December 9th, 1873, Thomas B. Cumpston and his wife 'who occupied good positions in Leeds' were arrested in a railroad station, in Bristol, England, charged with disorderly conduct, both of them in their nightclothes, Cumpston having fired a pistol. See the London *Times,* Dec. 11, 1873. Cumpston excitedly told that he and his wife had arrived the day be-

*Willie Reichel: *Occult Experiences,* p. 28.
**Victor Gollancz edition, London, 1931.

fore, from Leeds, and had taken a room in a Bristol hotel, and that, early in the morning, the floor had 'opened', and that, as he was about to be dragged into the 'opening,' his wife had saved him, both of them becoming so terrified that they had jumped out of the window, running to the railroad station, looking for a policeman. In the Bristol *Daily Post,* Dec. 10, is an account of proceedings in the police court. Cumpston's excitement was still so intense that he could not clearly express himself. Mrs. Cumpston testified that, early in the evening, both of them had been alarmed by loud sounds, but that they had been reassured by the landlady. At three or four in the morning the sounds were heard again. They jumped out on the floor, which was felt giving way under them. Voices repeating their exclamations were heard, or their own voices echoed strangely. Then, according to what she saw, or thought she saw, the floor opened wide. Her husband was falling into this 'opening', when she dragged him back." (p. 188)

"In the *Sunday Express,* London, Dec. 5, 1926, Lieut. Col. Foley tells of an occurrence that resembles the Cumpstons' experience. A room in Corpus Christi College (Cambridge University) was, in Oct. 1904, said to be haunted. Four students, of whom Shane Leslie, the writer, was one, investigated. Largely the story is of an invisible, but tangible, thing, or being, which sometimes became dimly visible, inhabiting, or visiting, this room. The four students went into the room, and one of them was dragged away from the others. His companions grabbed him. 'Like some powerful magnet' something was drawing him out of their grasp. They pulled against it, and fought in frenzy, and they won the tug. Other students, outside the room, were shouting. Undergraduates came running down the stairs, and crowding into the room, wrecked it, even tearing out the oak panelling. Appended to the story, in the *Sunday Express,* is a statement by Mr. Leslie – 'Col. Foley has given an accurate account of the occurrence.' " (P. 189.)

Fort uses the word teleportation instead of transportation. He is anxious to dissociate himself from spiritualistic or ghostly agencies. He quotes a report from the New York *World,* March 25, 1883, according to which the daughter of Jesse Miller, of Greenville Township, Somerset Co., Pa., was transported several times out of the house into the front yard, and adds: "But it was her belief that apparitions were around and most of our data are not concerned with ghostly appearances." (P. 182.) Similarly, "as told in the Cambrian *Daily Leader* (Swansea, Wales), July 7, 1887, poltergeist phenomena were occurring in the home of the Rev. David Phillips. of Swansea . . . . A woman of Mr. Phillips' household had been transported over a wall, and back toward a brook, where she arrived in a 'semi-conscious condition.' I note, that not in agreement with our notions on teleportation, it was this woman's belief that an apparition had carried her." (P. 183.)

Franz Hartmann, as an occultist, did not believe in transportation by spirits because such power of spirits did not fit into his philosophy. Fort, too, has his own system in which teleportation is a basic fact by which many otherwise unexplainable happenings can be explained. He says of stone throwing in poltergeist cases: "It may be that somebody, gifted with what we think we mean by 'agency', fiercely hates somebody else, he can, out of intense visualization, direct, by teleportation, bombardment of stones upon his enemy." (P. 41.)

Nakedness dreams, according to Fort, may be due to

the fact that "occult transportations of human beings do occur, and that, because of their selectiveness, clothes are sometimes not included." This thought is based on newspaper reports of strange naked men appearing at some places, bewildered and lost. He assumes that in such cases the dreamer woke up before he was teleported back.

The feeling of *déjà vu* (strange familiarity with a place as if we had seen it before), Fort places under this theory also: "It may be that many persons have been teleported back and forth, without knowing it, or without having more than the dimmest impression of the experience." When people claim to have seen a ghost that had vanished, he thinks the observers have seen a real man in the first phase of teleportation. "So many ghosts in white garments have been reported because persons, while asleep, have been teleported in their nightclothes." (P. 186.) Apparitions of the living are to be understood in the same vein. When persons have been seen "far from where, as far as those persons themselves knew, they were at the time . . . human beings have been switched away somewhere, and soon switched back." (p. 187.)

To explain teleportation as a basic fact, Fort advances this speculation:

> It looks to me that, throughout what is loosely called Nature, teleportation exists, as a means of distribution of things and materials, and that sometimes human beings have command, mostly unconsciously, though sometimes as a development from research and experiment, of this force. It is said that in savage tribes there are 'rain makers', and it may be that among savages there are teleportationists. (P. 41.)

This is a fascinating notion and a few things could be said in its favor. For untold ages, before we invented radio, insects had antennae and communicated by wireless waves. Teleportation of objects may be essentially an electronic problem. If it exists solved in nature, the technical solution may not be an unattainable dream. But Fort claims more than that. He endows Nature with a form of psychic life that reminds one of ancient notions of the existence of a planetary spirit. At that point his philosophy tails into sheer mysticism.

CHAPTER IX

Apported by Disintegration

THE vanishing and reappearing of objects with complete disregard of material and spacial barriers is perhaps the most universal of occult or psychic phenomena. Things that appear from nowhere in apparent defiance of scientific possibilities are called apports (from the French word "apporter": to bring).* They are not necessarily inanimate objects; quite often they are living things and, after a temporary daze, are none the worse for the experience. Hence the cows, oxen and horses that we have mentioned as transported by the Poltergeist also are apports. So is human transportation an apport phenomenon when the seance room is its mise-en-scene.

The fourth dimensional theory for the explanation of such spiritualistic phenomena as apports first was put forward by Johann C. F. Zollner (1834-82), Professor of Physics and Astronomy at the University of Leipzic, Germany, in *Transcendental Physics,* published in English in 1880. The book is an account of his experiments with the medium Henry Slade in which objects vanished and reappeared, writing was produced on sealed double slates (today a much discredited mediumistic demonstration), knots were tied on strings the two ends of which were fastened and other forms of penetration of matter by matter was demonstrated to the satisfaction of Professors Zollner, Fechner, Schreiber and Weber. Schiapa-

*See Nandor Fodor: *Encyclopaedia of Psychic Science,* London, 1934, pp. 11-16.

relli, in a letter to Flammarion praised the approach as most ingenious because "according to this theory, mediumistic phenomena would lose their mystic or mystifying character and would pass into the domain of ordinary physics and physiology." Lombroso shared Schiaparelli's enthusiasm and Flammarion also thought well of it.

The fourth dimensional explanation is not much favored by spiritualists who are responsible for the main body of observed phenomena.* They prefer to believe, on the basis of explanations furnished by trance communicators, that apported objects are, by an act of will on the part of the operators, disintegrated into their molecular elements without altering form, then passed through the interstices of matter that would normally block penetration, and reintegrated by a second exercise of the power of the will.

This immediately brings in a vast psychological problem. The operators, as a rule, are not claimed to be strange spirits wandering in the ethereal and dropping in for a call through the medium. They are permanently attached to their mediums and are called controls or guides. The outstanding controversy between spiritualists and psychologists centers on the question: are these guides or controls spirits of departed human beings or are they autonomous parts of the medium's own personality, trained to act and to believe themselves to be disembodied entities?

On the latter explanation the problem of apports would be confined to the medium's own unconscious.

*W. Whately Smith, later known as Whately Carington, worked out in *A Theory of the Mechanism of Survival* an application of the fourth dimensional theory to a wide range of psychic phenomena; but this early book is superseded by his later psychon theory in *Thought Transference,* Creative Age Press, New York, 1946.

Rene Sudre's construction that the medium's mind works on a molecular scale means exactly this. In all of which a tremendous assumption is involved: that beyond the solid, liquid and gaseous states of matter there exists a fourth, "fluidic" aggregation, a term which emerges as most descriptive from the explanation of the trance communicators. In this "fluidic" state, matter is conceived of as invisible and impalpable, possessing – conjointly with an expansion of volume – great molecular malleability, yet so inert that only by strong thermo-dynamic efforts can it be returned to its former solid state.

However, not all the communicators claim an unobstructed passage of matter through matter. Some say that a fissure or crack is required. As to dematerialization itself, an instance recorded by Ernesto Bozzano, one of the most outstanding Italian psychical researchers, seems to bear it out:

> In March, 1904, in a sitting in the house of Cavaliere Peretti, in which the medium was an intimate friend of ours, gifted with remarkable physical mediumship, and with whom apports could be obtained at command, I begged the communicating spirit to bring to me a small block of pyrites which was lying on my writing-table about two kilometers (over a mile) away. The spirit replied (by the mouth of the entranced medium) that the power was almost exhausted, but that all the same he would make the attempt. Soon after, the medium sustained the usual spasmodic twitchings which signified the arrival of an apport, but without hearing the fall of any object on the table, or on the floor. We asked for an explanation from the spirit operator, who informed us that although he had managed to disintegrate a portion of the object desired, and had brought it into the room, there was not enough power for him to be able to re-integrate it. He added: 'Light the light!' We did so, and found to our great surprise, that the table, the clothes and the hair of the sitters, as well as the furniture and carpets of the room, were covered with the thinnest

> layer of brilliant impalpable pyrites. When I returned home after the sitting, I found the little block of pyrites lying on my writing table from which a large fragment, about one third of the whole piece was missing, this having been scooped out of the block.

This is a very dramatic and apparently fool-proof story but it does not, by any means, establish the method as exclusive. In fact, during the Boston investigation of Margery Crandon, Malcolm Bird, then assistant editor of the *Scientific American,* reported a joke of "Walter", Margery's control: getting a mate for "Birdie." On November 26, 1923, a live carrier pigeon appeared in the closed dining room of the house. Walter, when previously asked where he would deposit the living apport, answered: "I can't say. I have to take a run and leap, and I can't tell where I shall land."

As to the question of how a living creature could be dematerialized without fatal consequences, advocates of the dematerialization theory answer that in human transportation the medium is always entranced, and that the body, by a temporary separation of the double (the vehicle of the spirit), is reduced to a comparatively inanimate object. A more simple explanation sponsored by trance communicators is that instead of the living organism it is the material barrier which is temporarily disintegrated, and the body is simply drawn through in a split second.

If only for the interest which it offers as a psychological document, it is worthwhile to read one such explanation *in extenso* as it came through J. J. Morse, a distinguished trance speaker whom W. T. Stead called "the Bishop of Spiritualism". The communicator was "Katie King", a picturesque spirit control, the daughter of "John

**Luce e Ombra,* August-October, 1927.

King" who claimed to have been in earth life Henry Morgan, the famous buccaneer. "Katie" was, at the time of this Morse communication, the invisible co-manager of the seances of Messrs' Herne and Williams of whom we shall hear a great deal later, and this is her explanation:

> The ceiling moves like a cloud. It is made up of little points of light. I magnetize the ceiling down to the medium. I was in the second floor when I made the link.* I can draw back the points of light. Magnetism makes them hot, like melting, and I attract him through the place; when I leave off the cloud comes together again. I could not do it in the light; the motion of the atmosphere would be too strong for me to overcome. John keeps the company going and draws from them earth magnetism, which helps me. It is a chemical experiment. The medium has to go in a trance, as he would be frightened if he were in a normal condition, and that would spoil the experiment. He passes as through a pneumatic tube, through the cone of magnetism I form. I wanted to carry Ted (Mr. Williams) outside, and have him come in at the street floor.

When the explanation was not found sufficiently clear, "Strolling Player" Mr. Morse's own spirit guide, took over, and this is the gist of his information:

> Modes of matter are atomic associations, the result of attraction and vibration. The harmoniousness of the vibrations being disturbed, the attraction of the atoms is overcome with repulsion. A space is thereby formed similar to fusion by heat. The same force produces solution of the continuity of matter, and envelopes the medium therewith, enabling the medium to pass through as if it were a tunnel. Immediately the medium has passed through this object, the activity being discontinued, the normal power of the matter reasserts itself and continuity is restored by reason of the atoms coming into their previous relations, and the vibrations being restored

*Messrs. Herne and Williams lived in a duplex apartment; the seance room was on the first floor. From time to time one of them disappeared and was found in the room above, apparently passing through the ceiling.

> to their normal action. The matter constituting the ceiling is elongated downwards, so as to form a funnel. With the atoms of the ceiling are intermixed the spiritual magnetism of the spirit operating, and also the magnetism derived from the sitters. The medium is pulled up by a kind of attraction, or suction, will-power on the part of the spirit operating being the motive force employed.

The editor of *Medium and Daybreak,* from where I take this quotation, (June 23, 1871) added a note: "Clairvoyants see a streak of light descend from the ceiling at the time a person passes through it. We confess the whole subject is in a very obscure state at present."

A candid and praiseworthy statement, for a good deal in the explanation reads like pseudo-scientific jargon. We do not know what the magnetism of the sitter or of the operating spirit is; nor do we understand the meaning "of the solution of the continuity of matter," unless it refers to the "fluidic state," the new aggregation of matter which the apport theory postulates.

However, the technique as of drawing the medium through a "pneumatic tube" or "tunnel" or "funnel" formed by some kind of instantaneous molecular operation emerges sufficiently clearly and holds a good deal of fascination, particularly when the mind or spirit is credited with the possession of the requisite power by virtue of being out of the body. For such a working hypothesis essentially admits that the force must be inherent in the unconscious of the living and that the state of trance may be the instrumentality whereby it is freed from whatever keeps it dormant. Calling the operation an act of will may be only a simple way of stating that the force is turned on.

Have we any scientific reason to assume that a biological force of this kind may exist? Or wording the question differently: is matter subservient to, or can it be changed into, energy?

In *Vogue,* Oct. 15, 1950, Sir Edmund Whittaker, a British scientist of renown, answers the very question:

> It has been shown that ordinary matter, visible and tangible, can be converted into energy, often invisible and intangible; and that indeed, the conversion of mass into energy is the source both of the energy which is radiated as light and heat from the sun and the stars. The discovery of the equivalence of matter and energy brought about a revolution in the whole conception of nature; for matter has previously been looked upon as inert and dead, whereas energy was the principle of activity; and now the opposite ideas had lost their contrariety and had become fused into a unity; the line of demarcation between the material and the immaterial was broken down.

With all assurance, Sir Edmund Whittaker declares that "all matter is energy", and that energy which is equivalent to matter "does not necessarily occupy any definite position: or as we may put it, some of the matter that exists in the world has no precise location anywhere in space."

Reflecting on such words, care is impressed upon us before we pass judgment on early attempts to explain the mystery of human transportation in such terms as trance communications reveal.

As to penetration of matter by matter, here is how Sir Oliver Lodge expressed himself in a controversy raging over the Rev. Stainton Moses' experiences:

> Now, whether it be surprising or not, it is nevertheless a fact that gases can permeate solid matter, for instance, a slab of hot iron; they can enter at one face and exude from the other, in large quantity and at a considerable pace. And in the process of osmosis it is familiar to chemists that some kinds of matter readily penetrate animal membranes, while other kinds do not. Even the common pro-

> cess of filtering may be regarded as a passage of matter through matter . . .
>
> The atoms of a solid are very far from being in contact, and dogmatic assertions as to the impossibility of percolation are rash. Besides, even if known molecular forces rendered it unlikely, the issue is not finally decided. Experimental evidence has given us a knowledge of three dimensions: it may conceivably furnish us with some indications of four.*

Further, as pointed out by Frank Podmore, an eminent critic of psychic phenomena** permeability of matter by matter is exhibited by the phenomena of crystalloid and colloid substances.

> These are names given to two states of matter, often readily convertible into one another, as when the colloid starch is converted into the crystalloid sugar, but yet presenting remarkable differences; for crystalloids can with readiness pass through animal membranes, such as the bladder and through colloids, whilst the latter are unable to do either the one or the other. Thus all our food has to be converted from the colloid state into the crystalloid before it is capable of passing through the dividing membrane into the vessels that supply the blood.
>
> In close connection with this is the curious fact, recently discovered by physiologists, that the corpuscles of the blood, little bodies about 1-40th of an inch in diameter, can pass through the walls of the capillaries, or fine blood vessels into which the arteries ultimately divide, without leaving a trace of their passage. Now the walls of these capillaries are absolutely structureless, that is, present no pores, or other openings, under the microscope, so that here is a real passage of matter through matter on a very small scale.

Electric action also is capable of producing penetration of matter through matter. As far back as Nov. 20, 1806, Sir Humphrey Davy, in his Bakerian lecture, detailed experiments in voltaic action "in which portions

*Borderland, Vol. 1, 337.

***Medium and Daybreak,* March 5, 1875.

of bodies were decomposed, and conveyed through other bodies in spite of the strong chemical affinity which existed between them, such as the decomposition of sulphate of potash and the conveyance of its sulphuric acid through a solution of ammonia, and many others of a like nature."

Metals also have been known as capable of diffusing into one another, not only when one of them is in a state of fusion, but when both are solid. According to Prof. Roberts Austen's Bakerian lecture "if clean surfaces of lead and gold were held together in a vacuo at a temperature of only 40 degrees for four days, they would unite firmly, and could be separated only by a force equal to one-third of the breaking strain of lead itself. And gold placed at the bottom of a cylinder of lead 70 mm. long thus united with it would have diffused to the top in notable quantities at the end of three days.*

In freak acts of lightning penetration of matter by matter also has been observed. Flammarion quotes instances in his *Les Caprices de la Foudre.* Here is a very early observation from a book entitled *The Stars and the Angels,* or *The Natural History of the Universe and Its Inhabitants,* published in 1858: "At a meeting of the Meteorological Society some years ago, I think in 1858, a paper was read by Mr. Andres Poey, the director of the observatory of Havanna, on the photographic effects of lightning, particularly on the curious phenomena of the photographing of objects that are near other objects struck by lightning. Mr. Poey stated the fact of lightning passing down a chimney into a trunk where without making any hole it left an inch depth of soot, which must have passed through the wood."**

**Borderland,* January, 1897.

***Spiritual Magazine,* 1872, p. 282.

These quotations have been taken from literature published at the time when the controversy over human transportation was particularly acute. Their purpose is to show that the advocates of the phenomena did not rely on faith or superstitious beliefs in their approach to the claims advanced and that the ground on which they stood was not as insecure as it first appears to be. If commercial teleportation of goods ever replaces parcel post, the process may be based on data discovered as a result of a careful study of transportation phenomena.

◄ CHAPTER X ►

Shifted Through Dematerialization

An old Negro melody provides a fitting introduction to the short range transportation of mediums, to which Spiritualists apply the dematerialization theory:

Such a gettin' upstairs
I never did see
Such a gettin' upstairs . . . .

In the description of how a human being, enveloped in some magnetic fluid, is whisked through a tunnel or funnel, no mention is made of how space is bridged when the element of distance enters into the problem. Like a kind of psychic intercom system, the short range transportation seems to be devised for getting a medium, sitting entranced in a circle, to the room above, below or next door and thus amazing and baffling the sitters over the power of the spirit guides who claim to accomplish the deed.

An account of Miss Ada Besinnet's transportation is recorded in *Light,* April 11, 1914, by "Paul" who, according to a note by the editor, "is a gentleman of high position in Canada, who for sufficient reasons does not wish his identity to be desclosed." He frequently contributed to *Light.*

> On November 19th, 1913, my brother and I arranged to meet the Z's at the house of Mrs. Moore (Miss Bessinet's adopted mother) and a seance was held at 8 o'clock P.M. in a room measuring 12 feet by 17 feet. We soon found that Ada's former manifestations of spirit singing, whistling and automatic writing, etc., described by Admiral Usborn Moor

> and Prof. Hyslop (who calls her "Miss Burton"), had given place to etherealisations, the direct voice and touches by materialized hands. At times innumerable spirit lights played about the table and in and out of the branches of the electrolier. It was pitch dark: the faces of the spirit forms could not be distinguished.
>
> The most astounding phenomenon occurred at the close of the seance at a quarter-past ten. My brother's left hand at the request of Mrs. Moore, had controlled the right hand of the medium all the evening. There had been a few minutes of absolute stillness in the room, when suddenly he announced that he could not feel her hand any more, and, at a moment later, that her chair was empty. Mrs. Moore exclaimed: "Then the seance is ended! 'Black Cloud' (Ada's Indian control) must have carried her to the next room; he does sometimes do so." The lights were immediately switched on. Miss Besinnet had certainly vanished; not a sound had been heard; the doors were found tightly closed as they were when the seance began; they were, moreover, covered with heavy portieres, running on noisy metal rings, which rattled when drawn back to open the doors. We passed to the next room and found Ada lying at full length on a sofa still deeply entranced; her hands were crossed on her chest and her features pallid and lifeless. "Black Cloud" had performed his task in the most complete manner. In fifteen minutes the medium awoke and was standing among us chattering, and apparently in a normal condition.

In spite of the endorsement by the editor of *Light,* one may object to the anonymity of the reporter. Hence we shall take a report by Prof. Pawlowski, concerning the Polish medium Franek Kluski, a professional man, poet and writer:

> The most extraordinary case related to me by the members of the circle is that of Mr. Kluski having been fetched by the apparitions, or disappearing from the sealed and locked seance room. The astonished sitters found him in a rather distant room of the apartment quietly sleeping on a couch. I

> report the case upon the responsibility of my friends, whom I have no reason to distrust.*

This is evidence by hearsay. We can improve upon it by quoting the personal experience of Haraldur Nielsson, Professor of Theology at the University of Reykjavik, with the Icelandic medium, Indride Indridason:

> We have had on several occasions the experience of matter being brought through matter, and one evening the medium herself was taken through the wall and into a room which was locked and in darkness. This sounds incredible, but many things occur in the presence of physical mediums which must seem absurd to men who have not themselves investigated them. But they are nevertheless true.**

The report of non-scientists sometimes proves psychologically more interesting. Willy Reichel reports on C. V. Miller, of San Francisco, by occupation a dealer in old pictures and Japanese objects of art:

> Mr. Miller was sitting in the cabinet in trance, when Betsy summoned me to the cabinet — "the German gentleman" she called me — that I might report this occurrence to the scientific world. There were 27 persons present at the time. Betsy told me, "We will now dematerialize our medium and move him to a room on the first floor and you and another gentleman or two must get the key of the first floor and bring the medium down again."
>
> Here I should mention that the house belongs to the medium and that the seances are held on the ground floor, while the first floor, Miller not being married, is kept securely locked up, as thieving is not rare in San Francisco. Betsy now requested us to join hands and sing in order to obtain perfect calmness of mind and complete harmony for this extremely difficult undertaking. The surroundings were again carefully examined, so that we were convinced that it would be impossible for Miller to get out of the cabinet without being observed by the 27 persons

* *Psychic Science,* 1925, P. 214
***Light,* Nov. 1, 1919.

> sitting directly in front of it in a light sufficient to see everything. Behind the cabinet a solid wall facing the street made egress that way utterly impossible. If any window should be opened — there was no door on that side of the room — a draft of air from the rainstorm then raging over the city would have been observed.
>
> In about four minutes Betsy's voice was heard requesting us to go to the room previously mentioned, the key of which I had obtained from the housekeeper, who was sitting in the circle. After climbing the stairs to the first floor, we came to the door, unlocked it, and found Mr. Miller sitting in a chair breathing heavily. I took the medium, who was still in a trance, by the hand and led him back into the circle, where he awoke, complaining about the pain in his heart, but without any recollection of what happened.*

The dispute over a natural disappearance through some architectural feature of the medium's own room is eliminated in the following report about William Eglinton, an English medium of colorful career:

> Last Saturday night, at a seance held at the house of Mrs. MacDougall Gregory, 21 Green Street, Grosvenor Square, London, Mr. Eglinton was the medium. The seance was held in the drawing room on the first floor, therefore high above the street; the shutters of all the windows of the room were closed and barred; they could not have been opened without admitting light from the street. The door was locked on the inside, and the key left in the lock. The table around which all the sitters sat, was about two yards from the lock and accidentally in the most favorable position for enabling all the sitters to gaze into the passage if the door had been opened either to a large or to a small extent.
>
> The members of the circle were seated around the table in the following order, in the dark, with their hands interlinked: Mr. Eglinton, Mrs. Fletcher, Mr. W. H. Harrison (of 38 Great Russel Street) Mrs. MacDougall Gregory, Mrs. Wiseman (1 Orme Square, Bayswater), Mr. George Southerland (of 117

**Occult Experiences*, 1906, pp. 27-28.

Sloane Street), Mr. J. W. Fletcher and Mr. Arthur Colman. After the ordinary manifestations had taken place, Mr. George Southerland was raised, chair and all, and placed on the centre of the table, where he was seen when a light was struck. Another sitter and his chair were raised about two feet. Mr. Harrison, half seriously, asked if the spirits could take Mr. Colman through the ceiling, by way of giving variety to the manifestations; this remark was spontaneous, no medium present having said anything to lead the conversation in that direction. Mrs. Fletcher and Mr. Colman then called out simultaneously that Mr. Eglinton had broken the circle and left them, and Mrs. Gregory told them to join hands. At about the same time a chair, probably Mr. Eglinton's, was heard to fall lightly on its feet, apparently some yards from the circle, and a violent "bump" caused by the falling of a heavy body on the floor of the room above, caused everybody to think that Mr. Eglinton had been carried through the ceiling, so a light was struck.

From the time the remark was made about Mr. Colman, to the time the light was struck, was about a minute. From the time Mr. Englinton disjoined hands, to the time the fall in the room above was heard, was probably less than ten seconds; some of the sitters a few minutes after the event occurred, estimated it at five seconds.

When the light was struck, Mr. Eglinton was not in the room. Mr. George Southerland unlocked the door, by turning the key which was in the lock; it was then noticed that the passage outside was feebly illuminated by reflected light, from the gas in the hall below. Mrs. Gregory and several sitters proceeded upstairs and found Mr. Eglinton lying in a deep trance on the floor, with arms extended. This was about two minutes after he disjoined hands in the room below. In two or three minutes he revived, and complained of the back of his head being hurt, as if by a blow; beyond this there was nothing the matter with him, and he was as well as before in a few minutes.

The sitters were all satisfied that the phenomenon was genuine, and that the door could not have been opened, closed and locked on the inside by any of the mortals present without their noticing it.*

The report fails to mention that two of the sitters, J. W. Fletcher and Arthur Colman, also were mediums and that a motive of rivalry may have been operative when Mr. Harrison, a science editor, suggested Mr. Colman's transportation.

An example of transportation of still shorter range is the emergence of Mrs. Salmon (pseudonym of Mrs. Carrie Sawyer) from a sealed wire cage in the laboratory of Dr. Paul Gibier (1851-1900), Director of the New York Bacteriological Institute formerly Assistant in Comparative Pathology at the Museum of Natural History in Paris. Here is his report, quoted from *Light,* November 16, 1901, of the experiment in 1898:

> The seance had lasted about two hours, when the voice of "Maudy" was heard from the cage; she said the medium's power was exhausted and the manifestations must now cease. Scarcely had she spoken when the bass voice of "Ellan" addressed me in these words: "Receive our medium who is coming out and needs your care."
>
> I thought it was time to open the door of the cage and release the medium, who since the experiments began, had been shut up in this confined space, and was about to light the gas, when the bass voice said: "Don't light up till the medium is outside."
>
> As I was not in the least prepared for what was going to happen, I stepped forward to open the door, the wire grating of which I could feel through the thick curtain hanging over it. At this moment I felt my hand gently but resolutely pushed back and the curtain swelled as though some form were pushing against it. I seized the protruding mass, and was greatly astonished at finding a fainting woman in my arms. I lifted up the curtain, we covered her and Mrs. Salmon – for she it was – would have fallen to the ground had I not supported her. I placed her at once on a chair, and the ladies present

**The Spiritualist,* March 22, 1878.

> came to her assistance with restoratives. Without losing a minute, while one of my assistants lighted the gas, I felt the cage through the curtain and especially the door of it, without discovering anything remarkable. As soon as all the lamps were lighted, we searched the curtains of the cabinet, which we found exactly as they were at the beginning of the seance. The covering was then removed, and we carefully examined the door of the cage, as well as the top and floor, and the wire netting. Everything was intact, including the dry postage stamps across the crack of the door, and the padlock. The padlock was in its place on the ring and locked. I took the key out of my right hand waistcoat pocket, where I had placed it, and unlocked it. The wards went quite freely and I was convinced had not been tampered with. Besides this, during the whole examination of the door I had not been more than a yard distant and must have heard any sound coming from the cage. Not the slightest noise or suspicious movement had attracted my attention, and especially when the medium was being pushed through the door of the cage, I heard nothing. Those present made the same assertion.
>
> This is the most extraordinary occurrence which I witnessed during the two seances which took place at a short interval in my laboratory, and a third at another place. Mrs. Salmon, however, would not agree to any further experiments with the wire cage, as it appeared to produce spitting of blood; and her guides or controls likewise forbade the use of the cage for test experiments and only allowed the wooden cabinet already described to be made use of.

These experiments took place in Dr. Gibier's laboratory. Here is what Dr. Gibier himself said about them:

> When the cage is closed with a padlock, it would be impossible for a strong man to get out of it with no more assistance than that of his hands. It goes without saying that it would be impossible to force an opening sufficiently large to admit of the passage of anybody through it, without noise or without leaving traces.*

* *Light,* March 23, 1901.

As to how the feat was done, this is the conversation that took place between Dr. Gibier and "Ellan", who claims to be a cousin of the medium who died 30 years before:

> Q. Have you brought the medium through the cage?
> A. I, and some other spirits who helped me with the materializations.
> Q. How do you accomplish this?
> A. We disintegrate the matter and recompose it.
> Q. The matter of the medium or the door?
> A. That of the door, of course. Living matter cannot be disintegrated; but it is easy to dematerialize the door of the cage, and rematerialize it.
> Q. Are you certain that living matter cannot be dematerialized? I know instances in which this has happened.
> A. Doubtless, you are right; only I did not know it. We have yet much to learn, and we discarnated spirits are willingly taught by you still in the body. There are many on your plane who are more progressed than some among us spirits.*

Prof. V. Tummolo reports a similar experience with the Italian medium Lucia Sordi:

> The cabinet consisted of a triangular space formed by a corner of the room and a sheet of gauze, 1 meter 70 centimeters in height, nailed to a wooden, U-shaped frame, which in turn was firmly attached with wax sealed ribbons to eyelets fixed in the two adjacent walls. In spite of such an impediment, however, the medium came out of the cabinet, leaving the wax seals and delicate gauze intact, and seated herself, while still asleep in the midst of us, and was so found by us when, on becoming aware of the phenomenon in the dark, we had turned on the full light.**

Finally we have a rather startling report from the *Sunday Post Dispatch,* Chicopee, Mass. (reprinted in

**Light,* November 16, 1901.
***Light,* Nov. 30, 1912.

Light, December 19, 1891), of an experimental seance of the American Psychical Society in a public hall at Onset, Mass., with Mrs. Etta Roberts:

"A large cage had been constructed of wire netting, stretched over a wooden frame work. This cage was built by a carpenter, who thinks he knows how to put wood and iron together so that they will stay. In the front of the cage is a door, hung on strap hinges, capable of being fastened with a hasp and padlock. This cage was set against the wall of the hall, which is on the second floor of the building, and accessible by only one door. Before the medium went into the cage her clothing had been thoroughly investigated by a lady who reported that it was of dark goods throughout.

"The audience consisted of 50 people, physicians and professional men among them. Mrs. Roberts entered the cage. Rev. Minot Savage, the president of the American Psychical Society, and a prominent physician having been appointed as a committee, proceeded to secure the cage.

"After closing and locking the door, the Committee took a spool of black linen thread and with a large needle passed the thread around the two sides and front of the cage, and in and out of the meshes, tying the ends in front, over the center of the door, and sealing them with wax, which was impressed with a private seal. All this was done to make it impossible for the medium to get out of the cage by any physical means.

"During the seance over 30 forms came from the cabinet, or materialised in front of it, in the space of an hour. Tall and short, stout and slender, nimble and stately, were the various forms that appeared, and were recognised by those to whom they went in the circle. The materialisation of some of these forms outside the cabinet was a most interesting spectacle. First a white nebulous spot would appear on the carpet in front of the cage. Gradually it increased in size until the nebulous mass began to assume the form of a human being, clothed in a delicate white drapery. The motions of the hands could be plainly seen manipulating the white vapour, gradually shaping it into beautiful raiment. At last the astonished people could see a human form fully developed, standing before them . . . . . .

"But marvellous as were these things, the most marvellous remains to be told. After a pause in the manifestations, the medium suddenly appeared directly in front of the cabinet, stepping out noiselessly and startling some of the company by her unexpected appearance. When the lights were turned up the Committee examined the cage and its fastenings. The padlock had not been opened. The thread with its seal was found intact. The cage had not been opened and yet the medium, who sat within when the seance began, was now outside. The theory given by the controls of the medium is that the door of the cage is dematerialised, or reduced temporarily to a nebulous condition, and after the medium is brought out, is restored again to its former state."

The problem of materialization is not within the scope of this book, but it has relevance to human transportation and to the passing of matter through matter as the substance called ectoplasm which issues from the body of a materialisation medium partially dematerialises that body. Thus Dr. Gibier's wonderment as to what is being dematerialised in order to get the medium out of a sealed cage has certain justification.

One negative element should be noted in pondering over all these short range transportation accounts: in none of them is any mention of luminous phenomena. In order to see this apparently rarer phenomenal aspect of transportation at close range, I shall quote here from two further records

The first is a letter from Joseph Briggs, Lancashire, in the *Medium and Daybreak,* June 22, 1877, describing how, in the presence of F. W. Monck, Dr. W. Brown, a private medium, was taken through the ceiling and back again:

> Suddenly the controlled medium ceased to speak and in the twinkling of an eye we heard him talking and stamping loudly on the floor of the room above us. Each person declared he had not moved, so that the medium could not have passed through our midst; those at the door declared that they had zealously guarded it all the time; and we afterwards found that had the door been opened only a very little, a flood of light would have poured into the room, at once showing us that the door had been opened. But no such light was seen. The door had certainly never been opened. The medium now came downstairs, and with some difficulty we managed to open the door and admit him. He was enveloped in a beautiful light. The sight was startling and awe-inspiring. He then returned to the room overhead and we heard him loudly talking and treading heavily on the floor above. In a moment this ceased, a momentary light was seen over the cabinet, which appeared to surround a human body, and in another second the medium was in the cabinet talking to us.
>
> While he was in the room above the large lights continued to play about the cabinet, and a slight female materialized form walked about and seated itself on the knees of one of the sitters.
>
> Dr. Brown was suddenly heard talking near the ceiling, and several of us put up our hands, and felt his boot in midair. He was floating about the room, frequently tapping the ceiling with his hands and as he floated over our heads, and while he was floating, four of us sitting in the sofa were lifted clear off the floor with the sofa.

The second account is modern and has a touch of

piquancy. It is by Adelbert Evian and it appears in his book *The Mediumship of Maria Silbert* (p. 104).

The author confesses that he went to the seance of this noted Austrian medium in order to pet with a girl in the dark. He lived in the same house where the seance took place on the third floor. After the sitting the medium did not come out of her trance and as Evian tried to enter his bedroom, the door opened by itself and Maria Silbert stood behind it, staring at him with green-gleaming eyes, her features stiffened into a lifeless, grey, menacing mask, flashes of light darting out of her body.

Cornered, he retreated into the sitting room, and she tramped behind him with machine-like steps. When she switched off the light, he bolted, and quickly double locked the door on the outside. Chuckling, he looked for his hat and was about to leave when the double locked door slowly and silently opened and Maria Silbert stood there. Mad with fear, he leapt for the hall door and got outside the apartment, retreating about 10 paces, keeping an eye on the door.

> Now, for the first time, I saw the medium penetrate matter, a thing that was fearful to look upon, because it was so unnatural and set all physical laws at naught. Later on, it often happened.
>
> As I looked at the entrance door, which was varnished in light color, it seemed to become transparent in the middle. At the same time I saw dull flashes of light through it. I sprang up a couple of stairs leading to the upper flat and sat down on a stair.
>
> The transparent-looking part of the door was somewhat darker, and the dark form of a body was visible, and a half formed head, about two metres from the floor. There were flashes of lightning, which became ever brighter and more distinct as if the door, which was my defence against the lightning, was more and more easily penetrated by it.

> Then the lightning stopped and I stared at the door.
>
> Yet again a powerful flash, and the medium stood in the door, not emerging from it, two-dimensional, as it were, as though her body had been projected, life size, upon the surface of the door like an X-ray picture. With bulging eyes I gazed at this phenomenon, which was new to me, and I rose, to be ready to run to the upper story. There was a flash, and Maria Silbert came out of the door-surface and moved towards me. The stairs resounded to her heavy steps. The expression on her face was, if possible, more distorted than before, and it was looking up. And now I lost my self-control; I took four steps together and ran up to the second story.

Unquestionably, Evian must have been in a very excited state and the feeling of guilt to which he confesses must have colored his story. His account is unique, as Maria Silbert, instead of passing through the fourth dimension, appears to have entered a two-dimensional plane. The only thing that approaches this in the history of Spiritualism is that in some materialization seances two-dimensional pictures were seen built up and photographed. It is a new angle to the study of the problem of human transportation and penetration of matter by matter, as it is much easier to pass a two-dimensional object through cracks than a three-dimensional one. The danger is that unless we stop we shall find ourselves at the Hatter's tea party where everyone was mad.

◂ CHAPTER XI ▸

The Flight of Mrs. Guppy

On June 23, 1871, at 61, Lamb's Conduit Street, High Holborn, London, one of the most remarkable instances of human transportation was placed on record. The event as claimed created considerable excitement and provided entertainment for editorial writers of the daily press. The "House of Mystery," as it became known, was besieged by crowds of the curious.

There was a seance room on the second floor and sleeping quarters on the third. The tenants were Messrs. Herne and Williams, two professional mediums in partnership since the early part of the year. They were fairly new arrivals on the spiritualistic horizon.

Frank Herne started his seances in January, 1869, giving clairvoyant description of the spirits surrounding the callers and telling them of their "aura." Soon noisier demonstrations, the so-called physical phenomena were claimed and these appeared to grow in power when Charles Williams joined hands with Herne.

It appears that Williams alone was not capable of anything spectacular. In fact, the Rev. William Stainton Moses, Master at University College School, London, one of the most remarkable private mediums of the day in whose circles Williams had been seen as a guest, doubted the genuineness of his power. But others were highly enthusiastic. At any rate, the partnership flourished and reached its climax with the celebrated case of Mrs. Guppy's transportation in deshabille over a distance of three miles. Here is the signed statement in *The Spiritualist*, June 15, 1871, that tells the story:

"On Saturday evening, June 3rd, at 61, Lamb's Conduit Street, High Holborn, London, W. C., a seance was held in the rooms of Messrs. Herne and Williams, mediums. Before the seance began, the doors communicating with the passage outside were locked. The proceedings began, at the request of the mediums, with prayer. Then spirit lights, like small stars, were seen moving about, after which a conversation between the spirits of John King and Katie King was heard. John said, 'Katie, you can't do it'. Katie replied, 'I will, I tell you, I will.' John said, 'I tell you you can't'. She answered, 'I will.' Mr. Harrison then said, 'Can you bring Mrs. Guppy?' There was no reply but a member of the circle urged that the attempt should not be made.

"Within three minutes after Katie had said 'I will', a single heavy sound was heard for an instant on the centre of the table. Mr. Edwards put out his hand and said, 'There is a dress here.' A light was instantly struck, and Mrs. Guppy was found standing motionless on the centre of the table, trembling all over; she had a pen and an account book in her hands. Her right hand, with the pen in it, was over her eyes. She was spoken to by those present but did not seem to hear; the light was then placed in another room, and the door was closed for an instant; John King then said, 'She will be all right presently.'

"After the lapse of about four minutes after her arrival, she moved for the first time and began to cry. The time of her arrival was ten minutes past eight. Mrs. Edmiston, Mr. Edwards, and Mr. Harrison went at once to one of the doors, and found it still locked; the other door could not be opened during the seance, because the back of the chair of one of the sitters was against it. There was no cupboard, article of furniture, or anything else in the rooms, in which it was possible for anybody to conceal themselves, and, if there had been, we, the undersigned witnesses, are all certain that by no natural means could Mrs. Guppy have placed herself instantaneously on the centre of the table around which we were all sitting shoulder to shoulder.

"Mrs. Guppy said that the last thing she remembered before she found herself on the table, was that she was sitting at home at Highbury, talking to Miss Neyland, and entering some household accounts in her book. The ink in the pen was wet when she arrived in our midst; the last word of the writing in the book was incomplete, and was wet and smeared. She complained that she was not dressed in visiting costume, and had no shoes on, as she had been sitting at the fire without them. As she stated this to Mr. Morris, and Mr. and Mrs. Edwards, a pair of slippers dropped on the floor from above, one of them grazing Mr. Morris' head; this was after the seance, and in the light. We all went into the dark room for a few minutes afterwards, and four flower-pots with flowers in them, which Mrs. Guppy declared to be from her home, were placed on the table at once.

"After tea a second seance was held. Within a single minute or two after the light was put out, there was a cry for a light, and Mr. Herne was seen by four persons falling from above, on to his chair. There were bundles of clothes belonging to Mr. Guppy, Mrs. Guppy, and Miss Neyland on the table, and Mr. Herne declared he had just seen Miss Neyland in Mrs. Guppy's house; that she had pushed the clothes into his arms, and told him to 'go to the devil.' The light was again put out, and when it was struck once more, Mr. Williams was missing. He was found in the next room, lying in an insensible state on some clothes, belonging to Mr. Guppy. He said on waking that he had been to Mr. Guppy's house, and saw Miss Neyland, who was sitting at a table, and seemed to be praying.

> "N. Hagger, 46, Moorgate Street
> Caroline Edmiston, Beckenham
> C. E. Edwards, Kilburn Square, Kilburn
> Henry Morris, Mount Trafford, Eccles, near Manchester
> Elizabeth Guppy, 1 Morland Villas, Highbury Hill Park, N.
> Ernest Edwards, Kilburn Square, Kilburn
> Henry Clifford Smith, 38, Ennis Road, Stroudgreen
> H. B. Husk, 26 Sandwich Street W. C.
> Charles E. Williams, 61, Lamb's Conduit Street, W. C.
> W. H. Harrison, Wilmin Villa, Chaucer Road, S. E.
> F. Herne, 61, Lamb's Conduit Street, W. C."

John King is the most romantic character of spiritualistic history. According to his own claim, he was on earth, Henry Owen Morgan, the famous buccaneer, knighted by Charles II and appointed Governor of Jamaica. He was the *spiritus rector* behind the violent type of physical phenomena of a succession of mediums from the earliest days of Spiritualism. It was, apparently, a mark of distinction to acquire him as a guide.

Katie King, who claimed to be his daughter, was an almost equally romantic character whose fame was founded on the seances of Florence Cook which convinced Sir William Crookes of the reality of psychic phenomena. But in the Herne and Williams seances there is some doubt as to Katie's identity as the daughter of John King as she once described herself as a descendant of the Negro race.

As to the participants to the seance, *The Spiritualist* says: "Mr. Morris is a Manchester merchant of high standing, and his sincerity in bearing testimony to these facts is attested by the editor of the *Echo,* as will be seen further on. Mr. Edwards is a B. A. of Cambridge University; he is a scientific man, and a few weeks ago he read a paper before the Society of Arts. Mrs. Edmiston is the wife of Mr. Edmiston, principal of the well known India-rubber establishment at Charing Cross. Mr. Harrison is a writer for scientific and other newspapers.

"The foregoing document was drawn up hurriedly, as several of those present had to leave early, to catch trains or to keep engagements, so we will now go a little more into details. The seance was held in a small room, size 12 ft. by 10 ft. 4 in., and it contained no furniture but the table, and the chairs occupied by the sitters. The table was of oval form, the two diameters being 5 ft. and 4 ft. respectively. The sitters and table so nearly filled the room, that there was no walking round three sides of the room without disturbing the rest of those present, and asking them to shift their seats. The fourth side of the room consisted of large folding doors, which were closed and which communicated with the drawing room. The opening of the small door of the seance room would have let in much light from the passage. There was no stool or anything in the room but the chairs of the sitters which would have afforded a footing to anybody trying to jump on the table. There were about two feet of space between the folding doors and the nearest sitter – Mr. Herne. Mr. Williams, the other medium, sat opposite Mr. Herne, at the other end of the longest diameter of the oval table; he was "sealed in" so to speak, at the further end of the room, by the table and the sitters.

"At the time of the solitary heavy "thud" upon the

table caused by the arrival of Mrs. Guppy, the members of the circle were sitting very quietly; Mr. Herne was talking and his hands were held by Mrs. Edmiston on the one side and Mr. Harrison on the other. When a wax match was struck, Mrs. Guppy was seen standing like a dark statue on the centre of the table trembling all over. The excitement, of course, was intense. The folding doors were closed; two of the witnesses noted the time, and three went to the door of the drawing room and found it locked.

"As Mrs. Guppy continued to tremble in the same attitude, and not to hear the words spoken to her, the candle which had been lit was removed for an instant, and John King said, 'She will be all right presently.' When she awoke, she had tears in her eyes and was greatly agitated. In the course of her statement about her removal from home, she said she was sitting by the fire with Miss Neyland entering some things in her account book, and while writing a word she suddenly became insensible. When she awoke in a dark place and heard voices around her, her first impression was that she was dead; then it flashed upon her that she had been carried to a dark circle, and she was afraid that she might be among strangers; finally she recognized the voice of one of those present, and felt much relieved at once.

"She complained that she had no shoes or bonnet to go home in, and was not dressed for an evening visit; while she thus complained, a pair of slippers (belonging to Mr. Herne we believe) dropped on the head of one of the gentlemen to whom she was talking, a minute or two later, a bunch of keys dropped into her lap before the eyes of those around her; this was in the light. At the short dark sittings which followed, a bonnet was brought and Mrs. Guppy recognized it as one which she had given to Miss Neyland a long time ago. Mrs. Guppy's boots and some articles of dress of hers were brought, also Mr. Guppy's overcoat, waistcoat and boots; four geraniums in pots about four inches high, standing in their saucers (one of the pots was upset, lying horizontally on the table); there were also articles of dress belonging to Messrs. Herne and Williams, brought from a bedroom upstairs. Altogether the articles of dress brought would have filled a clothes basket of moderate size.

"Once when a light was struck Mr. Herne was seen by four persons with his feet above the level of the edge of the table, his arms extended towards the ceiling, and his whole body falling with the velocity almost of a flash of light into his chair. He was moving in a curve from the top of the folding doors. He said that he had seen Miss Neyland, who spoke to him as narrated in the preceding document; also that he saw her in the billiard room of Mr. Guppy's house, but the billiard table had been removed from it, and elegant furniture substituted; he described the furniture, and Mrs. Guppy said that some of the things he described had only been bought and placed in the room that morning, also that Mr. Guppy had removed the billiard table to another part of the house.

"Mr. Ernest Edwards suggested that if Mrs. Guppy would grant permission, it would be as well for some of the witnesses to return home with her, to hear at once the statements of those at Mr. Guppy's house. Mrs. Guppy strongly approved of this suggestion. Mr. and Mrs. Edwards, Mr. Herne and Mr. Harrison accordingly went home with Mrs. Guppy in two cabs; the cabs kept close to each other all the way, and all five persons entered Mr. Guppy's house together.

"Miss Neyland opened the door. She was followed by

the whole party into the back parlour. No statement was made to her but she was asked, 'What had occurred?'

"She said that she had been downstairs with a newspaper on one side of the fire, while Mrs. Guppy sat at the other side of the fire entering household accounts in a book. The door of the room was shut. They were talking to each other, and on looking up from her paper after she had made some remark she was startled at seeing that Mrs. Guppy was not there. There was a kind of haze about the ceiling as is sometimes the case after strong spiritual manifestations.

"She looked through the downstairs rooms, and as she could not find her, went and told Mr. Guppy who was playing at billiards with Mr. Hudson, a photographer who lives in the neighborhood, and who had been helping Mr. Guppy in some amateur photography. Mr. Guppy said that 'No doubt, the spirits had carried her off, but they would be sure to take care of her.' Miss Neyland then searched the rest of the house, and afterwards she, Mr. Guppy and Mr. Hudson sat down to supper. Spirit raps then came upon the supper table, and the spirits said that they had taken Mrs. Guppy to Mr. Herne's seance. Mr. Guppy asked whether Mrs. Guppy was quite safe. The spirits said 'Yes'. So shortly after supper he went to bed.

"Miss Neyland was then asked, 'Had anything else occurred?' 'No.' 'Had she seen Mr. Herne previously that evening?' 'No.' 'Had she seen Mr. Williams?' 'No.' 'Where had she been most of the evening?' 'She had spent much of her time in the front room (once used as a billiard room) and *had gone to sleep there.*' 'What time was it when Mrs. Guppy was missed?' 'She did not know; it might have been about nine o'clock.' Mrs. Guppy here remarked that 'The clock downstairs was half an hour fast.' The whole party then went downstairs into the room from which Mrs. Guppy had been taken; her shoes were seen on the carpet in front of the fire, near her chair, and the clock in the room was half an hour fast.

"Mr. Guppy has since informed us that Mrs. Guppy came once or twice to him and Mr. Hudson in the course of the evening, suggesting that they should come and have supper; they replied that it was rather too early. He did not know what time it was that they last saw her.

"We regret to state that Mrs. Guppy was weak and unwell for several days after the occurrence of this manifestation of spirit power."

Two facts, not mentioned in the original account, caused considerable merriment in the public press. One is revealed by *The Medium and Daybreak,* June 9, 1871, an earlier account, according to which the last word inscribed in the book in Mrs. Guppy's hands was "onions". The second was published in a letter by Henry Morris, one of the witnesses to *The Echo.* When it was suggested that Mrs. Guppy should be brought, someone in the circle exclaimed: "Good Gracious, I hope not, she is one of the biggest women in London." *The Echo* published the letter on June 8, 1871, hence Henry Morris' account is the first that appeared in print. It is signed "Hy" but the writer's identity is easy to establish from the following editor's note:

> It is due to our readers and to our correspondent to say that we know "Hy" to be a Manchester merchant of high respectability. We should be very sorry to guarantee the authenticity of his narrative, but have no right to question his disinterestedness or sincerity.

"Hy" repeats that from the joking remark about bringing Mrs. Guppy to the time that she was on the table three minutes did not elapse. Aware, perhaps, that in the first signed statement no mention is made of the locking of the folding door, but only of the doors communicating with the passage outside, he explicitly states that the room was examined before the seance began and both the folding door and the other door leading into the seance room were locked. He states, "The possibility of her being concealed in the room is as absurd as the idea of her acting in collusion with the media."

During the second part of the seance, which was held with the recovered Mrs. Guppy participating, "heaps of flowers were strewn all over the table. Leaves from a horse-chestnut tree, with moisture on them as though just sprinkled by a shower of rain, and apparently just wrenched from the tree, were also brought in large quantities."

This additional statement is worth including as it indicates that Mrs. Guppy, a well-known medium in her own right and famed for her flower apports, was in considerable power — which contradicts the statement of the editor of *The Spiritualist* that she was weak and unwell for several days after her transportation.

◄ CHAPTER XII ►

Mrs. Guppy and the "Apport Post"

Mr. Harrison's joking remark that Mrs. Guppy be brought — no doubt motivated by the fact that she was an exceedingly heavy woman and hence her transportation would be a kind of acid test — makes it appear that the phenomenon was spontaneous. Evidence exists, however, that the event was anticipated and that, in a manner of speaking, a psychic rehearsal preceded it. Two weeks before Mrs. Guppy's strange journey through space, Frank Herne "dropped in" on her in an unusual manner. This is how *The Medium and Daybreak,* May 26, 1871, reported it:

> On Friday morning last (May 19th) Mr. Herne had called on a friend living at Caledonian Road. When near Thornhill Square, about twenty minutes past ten, he felt a peculiar sick sensation creeping over him, and he became unconscious and knew nothing till he came to himself at Mr. Guppy's house, situated at 1, Morland Villas, Highbury Hill Park.
>
> Now for the other side of the narrative.
>
> Mrs. Guppy was in her little breakfast room when she heard Mr. Guppy coming downstairs — this was about a quarter to eleven. She went to meet him and was in the act of speaking to him, when she turned round and between herself and the window saw what appeared to be a large black bundle descending from the ceiling. She screamed out at the unusual occurrence, when Mr. Guppy stepped into the room as Mr. Herne was arising from the floor. He had been brought there by some unseen power. Mr. Guppy's curiosity was very much excited, and he at once made a thorough search of the house to

> see if by any means Mr. Herne could have gained access. He however found three doors shut and securely fastened, through which any person would have had to pass before he could gain the inside of of the house. As Mr. Herne revived, his heart beat violently and he suffered much from thirst. It would appear that he had been carried by spirit-power between the two places described.

In answer to a protest by a reader who signs himself as J. N. Ogden, in the June 2 issue, the editor states:

> It may be that Mr. Herne walked in the trance, and was merely passed into the room by the spirit. At any rate, no additional facts have as yet transpired. We have questioned Mr. Herne and published his statement. We have also questioned Mrs. Guppy narrowly, and the results are in our paragraph of last week; so that we are at a loss to add anything to our previous statement. The window to the room was fixed down by special appliances, and all means of ingress to the house were securely guarded, as the doors and gate were bolted and locked. These were examined as soon as Mr. Herne was discovered in the room, and the bolts and locks were found secure. It is considered impossible that Mr. Herne could have entered the house in the usual way, and he can prove that he was in Caledonian Road a short time before he found himself in Mr. Guppy's house.

The distance is variously estimated from one and a half to two miles. There also is a slight variation in the time Herne is said to have disappeared. According to one account it was at 10:20 in the morning; according to a letter by Benjamin Coleman, a noted advocate of Spiritualism, it was 11:00.* Coleman was told the story the following night, at a seance at 61, Lamb's Conduit Street, and on the following day, he wrote to Mrs. Guppy with reference to Herne's "call" on her:

> You know that I have predicted that the spirits would someday carry *you* away, and this incident

***The Spiritualist,* June 15, 1871.

> with Herne led to my asking them, after we had taken our seats at the table last evening, if they could not return the compliment by bringing you to visit Mr. Herne and those there and then assembled.
>
> Presently there came, what appeared to be a preliminary arrangement, a suitable evening dress for you to appear in – a dress which I think I have seen you wear, black net, embroidered with coloured silk; measuring with a mantilla, as I ran it roughly over, about seventeen or eighteen yards.
>
> It is yours, I presume, because there was put into my hands at the same moment, a private letter addressed to you, which I now return herewith, and assure you that not a line has been read by me or anyone else. I should, however, like to know if there be anything in the letter which bears in any way upon the subject or the incidents of the evening, and in that event you will, perhaps, let me read the letter, upon which, for the purposes of identification, I have put my initials.
>
> Mr. Guppy, I hope, will take the trouble, if you have not the time, to tell me the exact facts of Mr. Herne's mysterious visit to your house; whether there were any doors open by which, in trance, he might have entered, or windows through which he might have been carried?
>
> A strict record of these very curious manifestations of spirit power may be of great value hereafter. The spirit brought, last evening, an ormolu table ornament, and an old miniature; the latter, I know, belongs to Mrs. MacDougall Gregory.

Benjamin Coleman's letter was answered by Mr. Samuel Guppy, the husband of Mrs. Guppy, on May 22, 1871, as follows:

> My dear Sir: I was on Friday morning on the basement floor. Mrs. Guppy was in the breakfast room adjoining, with the door open and had spoken to me. Suddenly she screamed, and said that something had tumbled down. I at once entered the room, and there was Mr. Herne on the settee, looking dazed like a person half-awake. When he got the use of his faculties, he said he did not know how he

had come, that he was going somewhere else, and in the street felt himself giddy, and knew no more. Our back-door was padlocked, our street door was shut as usual, and the windows were all closed. No servant let him in. It certainly is not an ordinary mode of making a morning call, although there are plenty of precedents in sacred and profane history of this sort of locomotion. The embroidered dress belongs to Mrs. Guppy, and was no doubt carried to the seance you attended by the same agency.

The letter was taken from a locked box in Mrs. Guppy's bedroom, and as it is an affectionate letter from a friend I enclose it for your private perusal. As there is ample testimony that Mr. Herne was carried out of one window and in at another, and also testimony of other persons having been carried by the same agency much greater distances, I do not see how the probability of this event can be contested.

Yours, etc. Samuel Guppy

Benjamin Coleman continues:

After the receipt of this letter I felt bound to treat the case as a serious fact, and to satisfy my own mind upon the subject, I went at once to Mr. Guppy's house to obtain further information.

The breakfast room floor is below the level of the road, and the only window of the room, looking out on a grass plot in front of the house, is for safety, screwed down and never opened. Mrs. Guppy, I was informed, was standing with her face to the window looking down at her needle work upon the table, talking at the same time to Mr. Guppy, who was washing out some chemical glasses in the adjoining room, six or eight yards distant, when she was greatly alarmed by seeing what appeared to be a dark bundle fall on the settee which is under the window. Her screams brought Mr. Guppy instantly to her side, and he seeing Mr. Herne, addressed him in strong language, demanding to know what he wanted and why he was there? This is the simple story, and the evidence is sufficient for me. Why should I doubt it after my recent experiences? I, and at least five hundred in-

> telligent witnesses resident in this metropolis, know for a certainty that windows, doors and stone walls are no barriers to spiritual forces. I have been covered with snow, white and pure, which no human hand had touched, whilst sitting in a room with the windows, doors and fire-place closed up. I have had put upon my knee a living eel, and I have heard of other animals being brought into rooms under similar conditions. The bringing of flowers and fruits into closed up rooms, and the carrying of heavy substances from one part of London to another by unseen agencies, are spiritual manifestations now of everyday occurrence. If this be so, where is the limit to this power? Believing in one series of such phenomena, I cannot discredit a well-attested fact, such as the one in question, and I do not, therefore, hesitate to say that I believe Mr. Herne was "caught up and carried away" in the manner described.
>
> Let me add that a very singular proof of this same power was given to me on the day I went to make my inquiries at Mr. Guppy's house. At the moment of our sitting down to an early tea – the sun shining brightly into the room – Dr. Dixon came in and joined us. In the course of conversation, I asked him if he had had any curious experiences lately? He replied that he had been but to one seance, about three weeks previously, held at Southampton Row (four miles from Highbury), with Herne and Williams as mediums, when his cap, which he always wears in a room, was taken by the invisibles, and he had not seen it since. None of us to whom he made this statement had been to that seance.
>
> Presently I felt something tapping me on the knee, and putting my hand beneath the table the identical cap was placed in it, and I restored it to Dr. Dixon. This was one of the many instances I have had of this nature which does not permit the possibility of any trick having been practiced upon us.
>
> 1. Bernard Villas, Upper Norwood, S. E.
>
> Benjamin Coleman

In another part of the publication it is made clear that these snow apports were experienced through Mrs. Guppy's mediumship. Further, Coleman says, at the house of a distinguished physician "some pieces of ice came down with great force upon the table; some of the lumps being the size of my fist and the quantity large enough to require the services of a man servant to carry it away on a small tray."

The editor remarks: "We were present when this occurred. Mrs. Guppy and her friends had been seated before a large fire for half an hour before the sitting began."

To continue Benjamin Coleman:

> All this while the doors and windows, and in some instances the fire-place also, were fast closed, and all possibility of external communication excluded.
>
> I have also had a living animal brought into the room under similar conditions; and very recently, in company with Dr. G. S. Thomson, of Clifton, we made a test experiment which precludes the possibility of mistake as to the presence of an invisible intelligent agent. We were in the garden, and just before entering the house for a seance, I suggested that some flowers which were growing should be marked; a string was accordingly tied around a lupin, the only plant of that kind in the garden, and a wire was twisted round one of the root of pinks. We left the garden together, and passing through the back-room and hall to the drawing room in the front part of the house, we seated ourselves at the table. Dr. Thomson having locked the door, and the identical flowers were, at our request, brought to us by invisible agency.
>
> The foregoing are but a few examples of my own experiences, whilst I have heard of others still more strange.

It appears that the incident of Dixon's cap also had been rehearsed.

In the Kilburn *Times,* June 3, 1871, is a long letter signed by C. W. Pearce, of 6 Cambridge Road, Kilburn, N. W., telling how he came to make arrangements on behalf of the Kilburn Society of Spiritualists for a series of seances with Messrs. Herne and Williams.

He called on them on May 26 at their home, and John and Katie King were consulted in an impromptu seance about the desirability of permitting skeptics to attend. Katie undertook to convince the skeptics.

> Just at this moment we heard a lump on the floor, and found that Mr. Herne was not in the room, and his chair had fallen on the floor, as if it had been lifted up and dropped down again. Coincident with the falling of the chair, we heard Mr. Herne's voice – as if he were at the end of a long gallery, filled with dense fog – calling out to Mr. Williams, "Ted, hold me!" Ted jumped, but he was gone. The room was empty. A few moments of conversation upon this wonderful manifestation when – lump on the floor dropped Mr. Herne, in his shirt sleeves, and panting for breath. After he had recovered himself we asked him where he had been. He said, up in the bedroom. John King and Katie had passed him through the ceiling with as much ease as if it had not been there. I said, "Where is your coat?" "In the cupboard upstairs," said he, "I remember taking it off directly they set me down in the room, and hung it up. I don't know why I did it." His slippers were also gone. Whilst talking about his coat, "John" said, "Never you mind about his coat, I'll get that for you," and immediately he dropped the coat through the ceiling, and it fell, neatly folded up, flat upon the table. Katie then said to Mr. Herne, "I'm now going to Lizzie's." Lizzie is a lady, by name Guppy, who lives at No. 1, Morland Villas, Highgate Hill, Park Road, about three miles from the place where we were. When Katie left I rose to go, but found we could not open the door. We, therefore, shouted for the servant to come and let us out. This she did. I turned to take up my cap, a soft tweed, from the chair just behind the one upon which I had sat, upon which I had placed it when I entered the room, and found it was gone. We concluded that when Katie said, "I am now off to Lizzie's," she had taken the cap with her. I therefore penned a card to Mrs. Guppy (a stranger to me at that time),

telling her the circumstances and asking her to write me if she found such a cap in her house. Whilst I was writing the card I was playfully pelted by invisible hands, and in the open daylight, with the tubes which had been left on the table, and also with some hanks of thick listing which were used to list the doors with.

I was hatless, and had to return from Lamb's Conduit Street to Kilburn – what was I to do? Mr. Herne lent me his hat, and settled the question. On the morrow, not wishing to retain his hat, I called on my way to business at Mrs. Guppy's to ask Mrs. G. whether my cap had been carried to her by the spirits. She received me very cordially, and told me that the evening I had written my card to her, she and a friend, Miss Neyland, were sitting after tea in her boudoir, or morning room, when she was surprised to see a black and white tweed cap on her sofa; she took it up and examined it thinking Mr. Guppy had bought a new one, but she saw it had been worn. She then put it away, expecting to have an application for it soon (it being no uncommon thing for her to have articles brought in the same way), and when the received my card in the morning, they looked again for the cap to see if it answered my description, and lo! it was gone. It had been taken away again. I had consequently to content myself with Mr. Herne's hat until the evening, when I again called at his chambers and found the cap had been taken back again by the spirits during the night. Mr. Herne saw it in the morning, and not knowing the kind of cap I had when with him the day before, thought it was Mr. Williams', but upon Mr. Williams refusing ownership, they both concluded it was mine, and it was. Thus ended my quarter hour's seance with Messrs. Herne and Williams, and I thanked God that however much blind materialism might attempt to prove matter was all and everything, and however much the new school of theologians may attempt to prove that except certain doctrines and dogmas of their own propounding be believed in, there is no immortality, I knew from demonstration that immortality was a glorious fact.

C. W. Pearce fails to note the most important question: at what time did the cap arrive at Mrs. Guppy's house? It is almost impossible to think that he should not have asked that question. We safely may conclude that no striking agreement in time was found or he triumphantly would have pointed to it as additional proof. On the other hand, if Mrs. Guppy had acted in concert with Herne, a more dramatic account of the arrival of the cap could have been expected. Yet this may be an idle mental observation for, as reported by *The Spiritualist,* June 15, 1871, at this time, and for the past six months, a kind of "apport post" was functioning between the Guppy residence, the house of Messrs. Herne and Williams, The Spiritual Institute of Mr. James Burn at 15 Southampton Row, Mrs. C. Berry's house opposite the Marble Arch and Mrs. MacDougall Gregory's home at Green Street, Grosvenor Square.

"All kinds of solid objects have been carried between these houses by the spirits . . . . The result of this is that residents in the said five houses are constantly receiving things without knowing to whom they belong and losing things of their own; this leads very often to letter-writing and frequently some little time elapses before the various articles reach their rightful owners . . . . At Mrs. Berry's house a white cat and a Maltese dog were brought from Mrs. Guppy's house by the spirits, the distance in a straight line being two or three miles. The dog seemed to be very much surprised and yelped and barked all the rest of the evening."

CHAPTER XIII

The Mediumship of Mrs. Guppy

It is now time to concentrate our attention on Mrs. Guppy herself and to learn a little about her personality before we discuss further her adventure at 61, Lamb's Conduit Street.

She was born in London in 1838. Her maiden name was Ann (Agnes) Nicholl (variously spelled with two and one "l"). She married Mr. Samuel Guppy in 1867. She now was known as Elizabeth, or Lizzie, to her intimates. After her husband's death, she married again and was known as Mrs. Guppy-Volckman. She died in December, 1917. The story of her mediumistic development is best told by an abridged version of an article in *The Spiritualist,* September 15, 1870.

According to this story, Miss Nicholl lost both of her parents before she was 11 months old, and she was brought up and educated by her grandfather, Mr. Nicholl, a sculptor of considerable eminence and ability. He was recommended by Flaxman as his successor as modeler to the King and he held the appointment for 25 years. While under the care of her grandfather, Miss Nicholl learned sculpture and became clever in the use of the hammer and chisel.

Her first symptoms of mediumship appeared at a time when she and her friends knew nothing about Spiritualism. When she was about nine years of age, she began to see spirits enter the room in which she was sitting; sometimes she saw them looking in through the windows. They appeared to open and shut doors, or to come through the wood of the door; sometimes they trooped into the room in such numbers that they appeared to fill it, and to occupy every available seat, causing her such terror that she became nearly frantic. These ghostly visitors were dressed both in modern and ancient costumes, and some of them, to use her own words, were "very funny, old-fashioned people."

By day and night Miss Nicholl was troubled by her fantastic visitors, who, however, seemed to be a friendly and good sort of people. Her grandfather alternately reasoned with her and laughed at her, in the effort to free her from the hallucination; finally he placed her under the care of Dr. Smedley, the superintendent of the baths at Matlock. Neither cold water applications nor plenty of exercise on foot and horseback in the open air relieved Miss Nicholl of her spectral friends.

Although she had been brought up in affluent circumstances, Miss Nicholl resolved for several reasons of a private nature, to perfect herself in photography and painting. She therefore made an arrangement with Mr. and Mrs. Sims, photographers, who resided at Westbourne Grove. A strong friendship sprang up between Mrs. Sims and Miss Nicholl; the former knew something about Spiritualism, and so did Mr. Sims, who, however, considered the whole subject repugnant.

When Mrs. Sims heard about the visions of her pupil, she told her that probably she was a medium, and that she might be able to get manifestations by sitting at a table. Miss Nicholl accordingly made one of a circle which was formed, and very loud raps were obtained; she would not believe that she had anything to do with the production of the raps, but found that when she left the table they ceased, and when she returned to it, they began once more. From that hour the visions which had troubled her for so long almost ceased.

A month or two after this, Miss Nicholl attended a dark seance at the house of Mr. Alfred R. Wallace.* The shutters of the room did not fit closely and admitted a little diffused light from the gas-lamps in the street outside. There, for the first time, flowers were brought into the room through her mediumship by the spirit, and showered upon the persons present. They were earthly flowers, fresh and covered with dew. They were seen falling in the dim light. The seance took place on December 14, 1866, and Mr. Wallace in an account about it published in the *Spiritual Magazine* on February, 1867, said:

> Obtaining a light, we were all thunderstruck to see the table half covered with flowers and fern leaves, all fresh, cold and damp with dew, as if they had that moment been brought out of the night air. They were the ordinary winter flowers, which are cultivated in hot houses for table decoration, the stems apparently cut off as if for a bouquet. They consisted of fifteen chrysanthemums, six variegated anemones, four tulips, five orange-berried solanums, six ferns of two sorts, one Auricula Sinensis with nine flowers, thirty-seven stalks in all.

The witnesses present were Miss Nicholl, Mrs. Sims, Mr. H. T. Humphreys, Dr. Wilmshurst, Mr. J. Marshman, Mrs. Marshman and Mr. A. R. Wallace.

The flowers were showered down, from then on, in profusion under test conditions, the medium's hands being held by those present, and the room thoroughly searched beforehand. Miss Nicholl met a certain Mrs.

*The great naturalist, co-discoverer with Darwin of the principle of evolution; he was a brother-in-law of Mrs. Sims.

M. Gregory, also a medium and a lady of distinguished family, in Paris. It was found that when they sat together darkness was not necessary; the flowers would fall upon them in broad daylight, and sometimes as they walked in the open air. The flowers fell softly like snow, and first became visible to the eye just as snow-flakes do.

Shortly after her mediumship began to attract public attention, Miss Nicholl went to the Mesmeric Infirmary, and qualified herself as a lady operator. She was highly successful in treating lady patients during daytime, devoting her evenings to spiritual seances.

Some of the most remarkable manifestations in the early days of her mediumship are on record in the *Spiritual Magazine.* At Mrs. MacDougal Gregory's house something heavy was deposited in the darkness on the table. It was found to be Miss Nicholl's own music box which she left at Hampton Court where she lived. The box vanished in the same mysterious manner as it arrived, and it was announced by raps that it had been re-transported home. Once a live dove was brought into the room; at another time the table and the dresses of the ladies were found, when a light was struck, ornamented with live butterflies – perhaps 30 or 40 in all. They were quite quiet and appeared to be asleep. On the leaves of the flowers mysteriously produced live insects and grubs sometimes were found. On one occasion a caterpillar was seen quietly eating a hole in a leaf, apparently in no way discomposed by its strange journey.

Long before her adventure in transportation, Alfred Russel Wallace, who knew Miss Nicholl as intimately as anybody else, reported levitations of her body. To quote from the *Spiritual Magazine,* June, 1867:

> My friend, Mr. Smith, who was a perfect stranger to all the rest of the party, sat next the medium and held both her hands, when her chair was drawn away from under her, and she was left standing. About a minute afterward I heard a slight sound, about as much as would be caused by placing a wineglass on the table, accompanied by a movement of the glass chandelier overhead, and an exclamation from Miss Nicholl. I saw something dark close in front of me, and putting out my hand felt a chair and a lady's dress, and on procuring a light Miss Nicholl was found seated upon the top of the table, her head just touching the chandelier. The table at which we sat was an ordinary round one, with a centre pillar and tripod feet. Miss Nicholl is tall, stout and very heavy. There were ten persons sitting round the table as closely as possible. Mr. Smith, who held Miss Nicholl's hands, declared that she simply slid away from him; and the next instant was found seated on her chair in the middle of the table, near which there was no other unoccupied chair; she was seated under the glass chandelier, where there was just room for her head, and yet this had been effected instantaneously and noiselessly! If any sceptics read the *Spiritual Magazine,* I beg of them to offer some explanation of the phenomenon. I pledge my word for the reality of the facts . . . . This remarkable phenomenon has now occurred to Miss Nicholl some half dozen times, in different houses in London, and there must be at least twenty persons of the highest respectability who can testify to the facts.

In December, 1867, Miss Nicholl married Mr. Samuel Guppy. In the summer of 1868 they went to the Continent and lived there for over two years.

At one of the seances of the Florence Spiritual Society in Italy, in a heated room, a thick block of ice about a foot square, fell on the table. Princess Marguerite of Naples asked the spirits for a prickly specimen of Italian cactus and soon afterward more than 20 of these plants were found on the table. They were removed with tongs, because if the spines of this plant enter the hand they cause much irritation and pain. Stinging nettles also were brought in a like manner. At the house of the Duchess d'Arpino a number of white flowers of a very unpleasant odor were brought. They had to be destroyed as they made one lady ill.

One evening, at another seance, the Duchess expressed a wish that some sea-water and sand be brought. Soon afterwards sea-water and wet sand were splashed over those present, and when a light was struck some live star-fishes were found upon the table. The sea was not much more than 100 yards from the house. Longfellow, the poet, asked for a sitting at Naples. As he held both of Mrs. Guppy's hands, several orange boughs were brought by unseen agency. He considered the manifestation one of the most conclusive he ever witnessed.

After her return to England, Mrs. Guppy acted as a sponsor of the Herne-Williams partnership when their joint seances began. In view of the fact that she could rise in the air by her own psychic powers, one can approach the mysteries at 61, Lamb's Conduit Street as a problem of three-fold co-operation, although Mrs. Guppy's role was not a professional one. While officially a sitter, her own contribution could be inquired into in the seance held at Mrs. Catherine Berry's house (*The Spiritualist*, June 15, 1871) of which we read:

> Mr. Herne was floated in the air, his voice being heard near the ceiling, while his feet were felt by several persons in the room, Mrs. Guppy who sat next to him, being struck on the head by his boots as he sank into the chair. In a few minutes he recommenced ascending, and Mrs. Guppy on this occasion determined, if possible to prevent it, she held his arm, but the only result was that she ascended with him, and both floated, together with the chairs on which they sat. Rather unfortunately, at this moment the door was unexpectedly opened,

> and Mr. Herne fell to the ground, injuring his shoulder, Mrs. Guppy alighting with considerable noise on the table, where, on the production of light, she was found comfortably seated though considerably alarmed.
>
> One of the circle now left, when Mr. Herne floated two feet from the ground in the light, and Miss Neyland was several times lifted up more than a foot, together with the chair on which she sat, a lighted candle being in the fireplace, on the same side of the room as that on which she was, so that the phenomenon was distinctly visible to all the company assembled.
>
> The following were the witnesses of these manifestations: Mrs. C. Berry, Mrs. E. Guppy, Mrs. M. Oliver, Mrs. C. Ellis, Miss Neyland, Miss E. Berry, Mr. Edward Ellis, Mr. Charles Neyland, Mr. J. W. Jackson, F.A.S.L. and Mr. F. Herne.

This is an important report as Miss Neyland, Mrs. Guppy's secretary, is seen to be a member of the floating circus. As such she must have been on the side of the angels. She was a medium herself. According to Miss Houghton,* she was hired after the Guppys returned from the Continent and Mrs. Guppy soon discovered her to be a powerful medium, although she was quite unacquainted with Spiritualism. She was clairvoyant but quite reserved and had not talked about her gifts. It stands in her favor that she made no attempt to make Mrs. Guppy's story more perfect.

Mrs. Guppy was 33 years old at this time. Mr. Guppy was much older and had had a previous wife who died childless. Now he had a child; Tommie, born during the Guppys' trip to the Continent and weaned just after their return on the last day of July, 1870, no doubt had absorbed a great deal of his dwindling stock of emotions. His family life certainly had many unusual features,

**Evenings at Home in Spiritual Seance,* London, 1881, p. 344.

not the least being that Katie, the spirit, functioned as baby sitter, rocking Tommie's cradle and waking them up at night if the baby was ill.

As no mention ever is made of the baby's transportation from one room to another (a frequent phenomenon under similar psychic conditions), we may wonder whether Mrs. Guppy was as fond of her child as of her flowers, and — generally — whether she was as good a housewife as the accounting book in her hand on the night of her mysterious journey suggests. With her manifold interests, her extraordinary vitality, the glamour of her particular form of mediumship and her love of experimentation,* she hardly could have been the type that settles down to household drudgery, even though her husband's means had considerably reduced that burden. One wonders whether her keen attendance at seances all over town, against the growing discontent of her husband, was not also an escape from marital duties or reality in general. There could be no wonderland more fascinating than the one in which she lived!

More important still, she was an orphan, although she grew up with a father fixation, grandfather stepping into the place of the original parent.** We find no mention of a mother substitute in her early life and it is quite possible that Katie, the spirit, answered her unconscious need for a maternal protector. John King, the ex-buccaneer, might have answered the father image

*It was through her instrumentality that F. A. Hudson, the spirit photographer, registered his first success; it was also she who produced the first materialization in England, which Podmore describes as a kind of Punch and Judy show.

**See letter from Mrs. Guppy from Naples to Miss Houghton, author of *Evenings at Home in Spiritual Seance,* London, 1881, p. 258.

for others, but she had no unconscious need in that direction.**

The spirit responsible for Mrs. Guppy's early apports is not mentioned by name. The plural "they" takes the place of a definite personality. But in Miss Houghton's book is evidence that Mrs. Guppy contacted John King at least as early as 1868 in a sitting with Mrs. Marshall, the first professional medium in England. We do not know, however, if Katie King already was in being at that seance. It seems that Mrs. Guppy had borrowed her from Frank Herne. Many others had done the same. Spirit "lifting" was a favorite pastime, and it still is, among mediums. Florence Cook, famous for having convinced Sir William Crookes of materializations, also contacted Katie at the Herne seances, although it is uncertain whether Herne had possessed, or was possessed by, Katie before he went into partnership with Williams, or thereafter only.

Assuming that Katie indeed was borrowed from Frank Herne in order to satisfy Mrs. Guppy's need for the supernatural parent, it also is reasonable to postulate that this fact would have established a strong emotional bond between her and Frank Herne, regardless of the latter's sex appeal. Mrs. Guppy, by her very size, could have been a "tremendous" mother image for Frank Herne and she, in turn, might have responded to him as a mother re-

**We have no evidence that John King or Katie King were disembodied spirits. We have far more reason to assume that they were autonomous organizations or splits in their medium's unconscious. In this connection it may be of interest to return to "Hy" 's testimony of Mrs. Guppy's flight and quote: "John King's voice was a very deep one, while Katie's was more like a whisper, but perfectly distinct. If you could imagine a moth flitting about a room on a summer evening, one moment striking the ceiling, and the next fluttering around your head, endowed with the faculty of whispering to you in its eccentric flight, you would be able to form a good idea of Katie's performance." Perhaps the reason for the lack of pitch in Katie's voice was the inability of the combined mediumship to produce a female enunciation.

sponds to a child when she sponsored his first seances. Such a relationship would permit a reversal of Mrs. Guppy's own role as an infant with her lost mother. It may be of considerable significance that the position in which Frank Herne "dropped in" at Mrs. Guppy's house was a fetal one. The motive of uterine return* might be the correct explanation of the libidinal situation that the newspapers joked about. A strong body-preoccupation on Herne's part could be suspected in that previous to Mrs. Guppy's corporeal arrival in a semi-naked condition, her evening dress dropped down on the seance table at 61, Lamb's Conduit Street. It is a pity that we have no psychological description of Frank Herne in any of the seance accounts. People in those days concentrated on the phenomena and not on the psychology of mediums. There is no reason why a male and female spirit guide should not answer the parental needs of the unconscious; just as partnership with a male medium might express unconscious homosexual needs.

Mr. Guppy quotes Katie that "conditions existed on that evening which enabled her to do that which may never occur again". What were those conditions? We might be able to answer the question if we knew the kind of revery into which Mrs. Guppy sunk before Katie whisked her away, or if we knew more about the psychic bond between her and Miss Neyland. Preoccupations about Frank Herne and about the many personal friends who were attending the seance at 61, Lamb's Conduit Street that night must have formed an important part of the conditions. The wish to be there instead of attending to dreary household duties may have sparked

*See Nandor Fodor: *The Search for the Beloved,* Hermitage Press, New York, 1949, pp. 207-230

her unconscious needs of escape. Benjamin Coleman's suggestion that one day she would be carried away had planted the seed for an unconscious anticipation, and quite possibly in some way she was aware that a big night was impending! Why then was she not dressed? Perhaps because consciously she feared and resisted the unknown.

She might have, of course, slipped out of the house, consciously, or in a state of ambulatory amnesia and she might have reached the scene of the drama in a normal manner. Could she also have entered the seance room and could she have climbed on the table in the same mental state?

The answer is: yes. Technically, it was yes even at the time of the event. *The Spiritualist* (July 15, 1871) publishes a letter to this effect. It is from an engineer who signs his name as T.V. and who was requested to make a professional survey. He said:

> The question I was particularly requested to answer was the following: "Was it possible for a person to have been introduced into the room, other than by the so-called spiritual agency, without being noticed by anyone of those present?"
>
> I am of opinion that it was quite possible.
>
> My reasons for arriving at this conclusion are as follows:
>
> Firstly. The adjoining room could be darkened so that on opening the door no light would be seen.
>
> Secondly. If a curtain had been placed before the door, light and draught would have been both excluded, whilst an entrance was being made.
>
> Thirdly. If the table had been placed in the centre of the room, there would have been sufficient space to admit of the door being opened wide enough for one person to enter.

> Fourthly. Though the doors made the usual considerable noise on opening, yet this would not be sufficient to attract attention during the noises which sometimes attend dark seances.
>
> I wish, however, to state that the possibility of a person entering is no proof that a lady was not brought through the ceiling; the probability resting in great measure upon the evidence of the assembled witnesses.

In August, 1934, I paid a visit to 61, Lamb's Conduit Street to make a diagram of the rooms if the house still existed. I found it still standing: a dingy house with poverty written in large letters over its apartments. The second and third floor had been made into two separate apartments. Mrs. Carter, who lived on the second floor, gave me permission of entry and examination.

I found that altogether there were three doors that had to be considered as places of entry. The two doors mentioned in the original signed account of the seance opened from the passage, one directly into the seance room (which was in the back and faced a yard, its single window being opposite the entrance), the other into the front room from the end of the passage, the front room being connected with the seance room by folding doors.

According to the signed statement of the sitters, "the doors communicating with the passage outside were locked"; that means both doors were locked before the seance began. After Mrs. Guppy's appearance "Mr. Harrison went at once to one of the doors, and found it still locked; the other door could not be opened during the seance because the back of the chair of one of the sitters was against it." While it is quite clear that "one of the doors" refers to the entrance into the seance room from the passage, the other door now refers to the folding door, and not to the door from the living room from which the folding door opened into the seance room.

This causes no confusion when the floor plan of the apartment is before us. More cause for criticism may be found in the fact that the sitter whose chair was against the folding door is not mentioned by name. It happens that it was Herne, Williams occupying the opposite long end of the oval table. The only man who was in a position, and had an interest to let Mrs. Guppy in clandestinely, was Herne. By sufficient wriggling, he could have reached and turned the key of the passage door (a duplicate key could have been used just as well if the original had been drawn off, or he could have opened the folding door for Mrs. Guppy. After the entrance, his own chair would have given her sufficient purchase to get on top of the table.

◂ CHAPTER XIV ▸

Two Men on the Wing

HOWEVER, in view of subsequent and previous events the question of Mrs. Guppy's appearance on the top of the table in the conditions described cannot be judged on such technical grounds alone. It is not sufficient to explain how she could have entered normally; one also has to explain Williams' subsequent disappearance and the statement that "Herne was seen by four persons falling from above on to his chair" when a match was struck. Further, one would have to prove that all transportations witnessed in that room on earlier and later occasions, were fraudulently produced. The only way to cover all this by a technical explanation is to suppose that a trap door in the ceiling opened into the bedroom above. But there was no trap door. Of that we may be positive. No investigator has suggested its existence. So the next logical question is: were Messrs. Herne and Williams ever caught trying to stage-manage a fraudulent transportation?

The answer is no. Both mediums have been accused, and legitimately so, of fraud at a later time, but on different grounds. Herne tried his hand at faking spirit photographs, Williams—after his partnership with Herne had been dissolved—tried to fake materializations.*

Harrison reported of Herne in *The Spiritualist* on June 15, 1871:

*Nandor Fodor: *Encyclopedia of Psychic Science,* p. 405

> I have been present, often in broad daylight, with Messrs. Herne and Williams, when solid objects, such as books and flowers, have fallen on us from above, where nothing but the white-washed ceiling was to be seen. Last Saturday morning I was standing very close to a bare part of the wall of the room talking to them, when a Bible and a book of poetry shot over the top of my head towards them; I turned round sharply; there was nothing but the flat wall close behind me.

Exactly a year later, on June 15, 1872, again in *The Spiritualist,* he published an exposure:

> Between two and three weeks ago, I first had evidence that some of Mr. Hudson's spirit photographs were shams, and that Mr. Herne had helped in the production of two of them. I soon afterwards called on the mediums with Mr. Blyton and Mr. Pycock; Mr. Herne came into the room once or twice, then put on his hat in a hurried manner and went out. I told Mr. Williams of the photographic trick of his partner, and that I should cease to attend their seances of the future.

We cannot tell for whom were these fake photographs produced. They may have been produced for Catherine Berry who, from the end of April of that year, records several experiences with Hudson's spirit photography, and ends up with this startling letter to the editor of *Medium and Daybreak:*

> Dear Sir, Just a few lines to inform your readers that last Wednesday at the studio of Mr. Hudson, 177 Holloway Road, between the hours of 2 and 5 P.M., and in the presence of Mr. Herne and myself Mr. Williams was seen to descend from the roof of the studio; he fell on the ground very gently. I do not think he was hurt, but sadly frightened. The spirit "John King" was rather vexed with him for not obeying a summons to come into the studio, and told Mr. Williams that this putting him through the roof bodily was done as a punishment, and he hoped it would teach him not to disobey in

> the future. We all went immediately to see if there was an opening in the roof, but there was none, and the boards had all the appearance of not having been disturbed. After this we tried for a spirit photograph, but could not succeed because of the mediums having been excited.*

A planned, fraudulent demonstration should have succeeded as the excitement would have diverted vigilance. The wording that "Williams was seen to descend" and the further statement that "he fell on the ground very gently" suggests that his arrival took place in full visibility, or at least that the last stage of his arrival was similar to Herne's at Mrs. Guppy's residence.

In another account *(The Medium and Daybreak,* June 30, 1871), we are told that Williams disappeared during a seance he and Herne gave to J. J. Morse and Mrs. Burns at 61, Lamb's Conduit Street.

"After a few unimportant manifestations, the chairs of the three sitters were forcibly drawn from under them and placed upon the table. Two of the chairs were then taken off the table and placed upon Mr. Williams' head and shoulders, when all at once Mrs. Burns felt his hand pulled forcibly from hers, and Mr. William's body seemed to pass upwards through the chairs, which came clattering to the ground very noisily. Mrs. Burns exclaimed, 'Williams has gone'. Search was made for him which terminated unsuccessfully. They then joined hands awaiting further results.

"After a short time, spirit lights were observed, and a musical box began to play, floating around the room, and at times being placed upon the hands of the sitters, when presently the noise of a heavy body falling resounded through the room, which was found to be Mr. Wil-

*Catherine Berry: *Experiences in Spiritualism,* London, 1876, pp. 191-192

liams returned. He exclaimed, 'Where am I?' The voices of the spirits 'Katie' and 'John' talked to the sitters for a little, when all at once Mr. Herne was lifted with great violence; he was heard to say, 'Oh, for God's sake, take me up or put me down.' The voice of 'Katie' in derision replied, 'John is a muff at passing them through the ceiling; he thinks he is clever; why don't he let me do it? He is trying to find a soft place in the ceiling to put him through,' finishing the sentence by laughing at 'John's' awkwardness. Mrs. Burns then suggested that 'Katie' should help him, when she replied, 'I won't, I won't; he would not help me when I carried Lizzie (Mrs. Guppy) and said I could not do it, but I did, and now he may do his own work himself.'

"Mr. Herne was then taken up and a noise was heard overhead. In about a minute Mr. Herne was brought back again, when he said, 'He passed me through that cupboard right up into the other room and back again.' Mr. Herne's coat and waistcoat were then taken off by the spirit, and laid on a chair that was standing upon the table while all hands were joined. Suddenly Mr. Herne was pulled up again. Mrs. Burns felt for the coat and waistcoat, but they could not be found. A search was made for Mr. Herne, but he was not to be found in the room. In less than a minute something dropped near to Mr. Morse, who felt Mr. Herne in his shirt-sleeves. Mr. Herne was asked what he had done with his coat and waistcoat. He replied, 'I do not know.'

"The four sat down again and joined hands, the doors being all the while locked. 'John's' voice was heard imploringly saying, 'Oh, Katie, what are you up to? You had better not do it.' He continued to expostulate with her, but 'Katie' told him to mind his own business, when

'John' cried, 'Look out, here is something coming', when down came a large soft body upon the heads of the company, nearly smothering them. A light was immediately struck, when it was found that a large feather bed had been brought out of the front room on the floor above.

"The seance was at once broken up, and Mr. Herne, assisted by Mr. Williams, proceeded to carry the bed upstairs, Mr. Williams declaring that 'Katie' must be inside of it, as it was so heavy. Immediately upon their getting the bed into the bedroom, Mr. Herne was heard to exclaim, 'Come upstairs, Mrs. Burns and Mr. Morse—they have taken Ted away.'

"Mrs. Burns and Mr. Morse at once ran upstairs, when Mr. Herne said, 'While putting the bed upon the bedstead I felt the power come and take hold of Ted, and I saw him whisked through the wardrobe. As they have taken him out of this room, we had better sit here, so perhaps they will bring him back again.'

"The audible voice was heard to say, 'Go down into the seance room.' The bedroom was thoroughly searched, and on going downstairs the front room and the seance room were also searched. Then they darkened the seance room, closed and locked the doors of both rooms, taking hold of hands, and standing up in the dark room with their backs to the folding door. After standing about a minute, Mr. Herne, Mrs. Burns and Mr. Morse exclaimed simultaneously, 'Oh, look there, do you see that long stream of light (as it were a narrow sheet of water falling from the ceiling)? Oh, there is Williams' who was seen suspended in this stream of light for some time, his feet being about two feet from the floor. Mr. Williams was spoken to while thus suspended, but he did not reply till his feet touched the floor. He was again asked, 'Williams, is that you?' He replied, 'Yes.' 'Where have you been to?' He replied, 'I think I saw some sky and trees.' They asked 'Katie' where she had taken him; she replied, 'To Lizzie's (Mrs. Guppy's) but they did not see him.'

"The seance was then broken up and as they stood talking in the front room, in broad daylight, two hats, one belonging to Mr. Herne and one to Mr. Williams, which had been seen in the bedroom above when search was being made for Mr. Williams, were thrown at the party. Flowers were taken from the vases upon the mantel shelf, and thrown at them as they stood in the light. The cashbox that was standing upon the sideboard was taken up and thrown in their midst as they stood in conversation. Books and other objects were taken from the table and strewn about the room by the same invisible agency, and the audible voice was heard speaking. These latter manifestations occurred in a well-lighted room in the afternoon."

The report is concluded by the following editorial remark:

> The utmost reliance may be placed in the foregoing account. The spirit "John King" called it a "rehearsal". The phenomena were very remarkable but it must be remembered that the company consisted of four persons, all mediums. From this and many other incidents that occur to these mediums in private, it appears that these wonderful manifestations may and do occur in light. The above particulars are given as fully as possible, that the reader may realize exactly the conditions under which the remarkable phenomena took place. The utmost scrutiny was exercised by all, Messrs. Herne and Williams being as curious to investigate the matter as strangers are.

The outstanding part of this story is the vision of a

narrow sheet of light which, on descending from the ceiling, turned into Williams. The moral standing of J. J. Morse was so high that the question of deliberate misrepresentation or complicity can be ruled out. Neither mal-observation nor over-imagination accounts for all the phenomena of the report. As the seance took place on June 20 and the report was published 10 days afterwards, we may assume that it was drawn up almost immediately, so that the objections of memory playing tricks also may be excluded.

That objection may well be sustained in case of reminiscences as by Thomas Blyton in *Light,* April 11, 1931:

> I was present on one occasion at a private home seance at Hackney in London, when without warning or preparation, in total darkness, Mr. Frank Herne was suddenly placed in the midst of the sitters; and after recovering from our surprise and resuming the seance, Mr. Herne's overcoat, hat and umbrella were dropped on the table. John King, speaking in the direct voice, explained that his band of spirit people had found an unexpected opportunity to transport Mr. Herne from where he had been with friends, witnessing a theatrical play that evening; on his appearance at Hackney he was in a semi-conscious condition.

One would expect that Herne's disappearance from the auditorium of a theatre was sufficiently startling to be bruited about in the spiritualistic press. However, I was unable to find any references to this additional wonder in contemporary publications.

CHAPTER XV

Snatched Up in the Spirit Net

THAT SPIRIT John King could cast a wide net for mediums appears from the story of Miss Lottie Fowler's adventure as told in *The Medium and Daybreak,* February 23, 1872. According to a letter to the editor, signed by H. Clifford Smith, Miss Lottie Fowler always turned a deaf ear to stories of the marvelous phenomena which occur under physical mediumship. Being exclusively a mental medium, she considered the carrying of objects, and far more, the carrying of the human body from place to place, an impossibility, and every mention of any such thing met with her utmost incredulity. "This," wrote H. Clifford Smith, "renders the phenomenon or manifestation which I witnessed on Saturday night, the 17th of February, the more remarkable.

"At the usual time I went to the house of Messrs. Herne and Williams, to attend their customary Saturday evening seance. A few friends, with whom I have frequently sat on former occasions, were present, and a gentleman and lady whom I do not remember to have met previously. With the mediums, the number who entered the seance-room (which has been so frequently described with reference to the aerial transport of Mrs. Guppy) was eight. Having taken our seats, Mr. Williams proceeded to close the folding doors, leaving the gas burning brightly in the front-room. He locked the doors and handed the key to a lady who was present. He then took his seat and we waited in the usual manner, little expecting what was about to take place.

"Two minutes could not have elapsed before I felt the passage of some drapery overhead, and directly afterwards all exclaimed that some person was on the table, and various conjectures were made as to the person it could be; this could only be decided when a light was obtained, when I, who was nearest to her face, recognized her as Miss Lottie Fowler. She was in a deep trance. The pulse, however, which I felt immediately, was full, but rapid and fluttering, as a person's under the influence of great excitement. Afterwards this subsided and became gradually weak and feeble, but rapid, as in a person in an extreme state of exhaustion.

"During her trance, she was frequently influenced by a spirit, 'Annie', who spoke distinctly in her own characteristic way, and endeavored to describe the manner in which she was brought. She stated that her medium would sleep and remain in the trance condition until half past eight, but that we were to continue sitting and wait for further manifestations. It would take me too long to enter into all the interesting particulars of the seance, or of the conversation held with 'Annie'. Suffice it to say that Miss Fowler with some difficulty recovered consciousness at half past eight precisely. The time, which I carefully noted, when she was so suddenly brought into our midst, was a quarter past seven.

"Miss Fowler when she awoke from her trance became exceedingly excited – would not credit what had happened, but seemed rather more willing to accept the idea that she herself was mad, and it was long ere she would listen to anyone who tried to assure her of the fact of her perfect sanity.

"When she was come sufficiently to herself she gave the same account of herself which the spirit 'Annie' had previously given – to the effect that she had left her home in Keppel Street, Russel Square, at seven o'clock, proceeded to the corner of Tottenham Court Road, and there entered an omnibus going up Oxford Street, as she was on her way to Mrs. Gregory's. She felt sick but that was all that she could call to memory; she knew nothing more until after her return to consciousness in our midst. I think, notwithstanding all her previous obstinacy, she will in future credit the spirits with the power of carrying not only lighter objects, but also herself."

In spite of the frequency with which John and Katie King demonstrated their uncanny ability to snatch people away, their missionary effort failed. The spiritualists were convinced, but the world-at-large refused to take notice. On no occasion was this made clearer than when their next startling coup was performed, this time in the Guppy home at 1 Moreland Villas, Highbury. The victim, a well-known photographer, was a skeptic, a Saul among the spiritualists. He was carried from the locked seance room to a stable at 29 Kingsdown Road, a distance of a mile and a half. The design might have been to deposit him as a companion to a horse inside the stable, but the power failed and he was dropped on the roof from which he rolled off into the yard, creating considerable commotion.

The photographer is called Mr. Blank and only years later was his identity as Mr. A. L. Henderson revealed. The date of the event was November 2, 1873. On November 14 a long and detailed report, with the names of all the participants of the seance affixed, was submitted to the *Daily Telegraph,* the *Standard* and the *Daily*

News, but publication was flatly refused. As a result, the report saw the light only in the December 5 issue of *The Medium and Daybreak.*

We omit the preliminaries about the locking of the door, with the key being left inside and the curtains carefully drawn, and begin at the point where the sitters, directed by raps, were asked to wish for something. They expressed their desires as follows: Mrs. Guppy that someone might be carried out of the room; Mr. Fisher for some cigarettes, five of which were brought; Mrs. Fisher for some pencils, three of which were brought; Mr. Guppy for some grapes, a bunch being brought as also were some walnuts presumably at the request of Mr. Volckman for fruit.

The report continues: "After these events, which occurred while all present were holding hands, a very violent rocking of the table commenced and was continued for some little while during which time chairs were removed from under two of the visitors (Mrs. Fisher and Mr. Blank) and were heard to be moving about the room. By reason of the violent movement of the somewhat cumbrous table we had much difficulty in maintaining an unbroken circle and some of us now and again momentarily lost hold of each other's hands. We had kept up, however, an animated conversation when to the general surprise both the voice and hands of Mr. Blank were suddenly missed, he having ceased to answer us notwithstanding our repeated calls to him. Whereupon a light was struck, and the fact revealed that no Mr. Blank was in the room. More than ten minutes could not have elapsed since the last time the gas had been extinguished to the moment of discovering Mr.

Blank's absence, while from first to last we estimate the sitting as of twenty minutes' duration.

"All eyes turned instinctively to the door and it was at once observed that the table covering placed at its foot, to exclude the light, was undisturbed although the door opens into the room. The handle of the door was then tried but only to assure the party that the door was still locked, the key being found in the lock in the inside of the room as left at the commencement of the seance. The windows also were found closed and the shutters thereof duly fastened to the satisfaction of all present. The house and garden were then searched, but the only further discovery made was that Mr. Blank's great coat and hat were also missing, but not his umbrella. Mrs. Blank shortly after this search, and fearing to lose the last train, took her leave at about half past ten o'clock and about fifteen or twenty minutes after her husband's disappearance, taking his umbrella with her. The remainder of the party then stood at the table in the light, and were informed by raps that Mr. Blank was a considerable distance off, had been carried away, and would not be seen by us that evening.

"It is necessary here to add that the room in question contains no means of egress or entrance other than the door, the chimney and the windows, and is devoid of lengthy curtains, cupboards or other means of concealment. Its walls were papered throughout some three months ago and its floor is covered over the entire area with a carpet (nailed down at the edges in the ordinary manner) upon which again are two pieces of druggeting also firmly nailed down and presenting no traces of recent disturbance. It must also be stated that the door of the room could not have been opened during the seance without detection through the letting in of light; for the room-door faces the street-door which has glass panels and the nearly-full moon was affording considerable light notwithstanding the cloudy and wet weather prevailing on the night in question.

"So far we have concisely stated our own experiences as confined to the sitting-room at Highbury. We now proceed to record the statement we have received from Mr. Blank, as made by him partially by letter and afterwards in full detail to the various members of the seance individually and collectively. This statement (given to us by Mr. Blank under promise that we should not divulge his name in any report we might publish) is briefly as follows:

"That Mr. Blank has a full remembrance of the seance above recorded, his last impression of it being the violent rocking of the table. That his next impression was one of semi-consciousness, in which condition he felt himself as rolling from off a roof, his left hand tightly grasping something. That in a dazed and confused state he then found himself on his feet in a paved yard surrounded by walls and outhouses. That he tried a door which entered into a stable where was a horse. That on trying another door he was assailed by cries of 'Police', that voices from a window or roof above him then accosted him asking 'Who he was? What he did there?' etc., etc. That he replied by asking 'Who are you? Where am I? I'm not drunk', and so on.

"That his voice was then recognized by the persons to whom he was speaking, who immediately addressed him by his name and let him into the house by way of the yard door. That he then found himself in the presence of Mr. and Mrs. Stokes and family (recent acquaintances of his) in their house at No. 29 Kingsdown Road, Holloway. That the family had just finished supper, the time being five minutes after ten o'clock. That during supper he had been a subject of their conversation.

"That as soon as he had sufficiently recovered himself from his nervous condition he told them of the seance at Highbury and *that he was wholly unconscious of how he got into their premises;* That they examined his clothes and found them free from such moisture as might reasonably have been expected on such a rainy night, his boots, except under the soles thereof, being soiled by dry mud only, and presenting no traces of recent walking or running. That his face, however, was pallid and covered with perspiration. That his breathing was not unusually rapid. That a stain of reddish-brown paint was found on his left hand. That he had on his grey coat and hat. That he made inquiries for his umbrella which could not be found. That he was informed by Mr. Stokes' stable-boy that the distance between Highbury and Kingsdown Road was two miles. That after staying a short time to refresh himself, he departed, and by cab and tram-car reached his home where he found his wife had arrived about half an hour previously and in a state of much alarm.

"This statement Mr. Blank consistently maintains, especially and repeatedly emphasizing the fact *that as to his transit from within the sitting-room at Highbury to within the stable-yard at Kingsdown Road he has not the smallest knowledge or reminiscence.* But the writers of this letter, desiring to judge for themselves, sought direct testimony to all such parts of Mr. Blank's statement as it was possible for Mr. Stokes and his family to verify or contradict. Accordingly, three of the sitters paid an early visit, without appointment, to 29 Kingsdown Road, were received by Mr. and Mrs. Stokes and were permitted to examine the stable-yard and surroundings of Mr. Blank's arrival.

"The house (which they estimate as one mile and a half from the house at Highbury) is a corner one, and its stable-yard abuts a side street running out of Kingsdown Road being enclosed on the street-side by a brick wall varying from six to eight feet high and on the other sides by the adjoining houses and their gardens. The stable roof may easily be reached from the street steps, is about nine feet high at the eaves, and adjoins the roof of another outhouse about seven feet high at the eaves, both roofs being skirted by a metal gutter painted in a reddish-brown colour. The sum-total of their inquiries amounts to the corroboration in all essential particulars of Mr. Blank's statement as above rendered and to which they are enabled to add Mr. Stokes' assurance that he tried and found his yard gate to be duly locked at the time of the discovery of Mr. Blank on his premises. In confirmation of these particulars and of Mr. Blank's statement in general, and also as an emphatic declaration by Mr. Stokes and family of *no collusion* between themselves and Mr. Blank or any other person whatever in this matter, we have the pleasure to be able to append the names of nine witnesses signed by themselves (being all the persons who have direct knowledge of Mr. Blank's arrival and discovery as above detailed) viz:

Joiner Stokes	Edward Bullock (stable-boy)
Alice Stokes	Emma Cotton (servant)
Lizzie Stokes	William Mannion
Kate Stokes	Charlotte Mannion (per W.M., her husband)
Florence Stokes	

All of No. 29 Kingsdown Road.

"Beyond these nine witnesses no adults were in the house; but two children, the one two and a half years and the other five and a half years old, were in bed. We are also informed that Mr. Stokes and family are investigators of the phenomena alleged to be spiritual, and occasionally hold seances at which curious manifestations sometimes occur. They had not, however, been sitting on the evening in question, are not professional mediums or employers of public mediums, but rely for mediumship, so-called, upon their own family circle.

"In thus faithfully recording the salient feature of this strange occurrence we (the writers of this report) have no wish to obtrude, or give prominence to, any theory of our own in explanation, but would merely venture such comments as naturally arise out of this event, especially as taken in connection with the alleged transference of Mrs. Guppy on June 3d, 1871. On that occasion the solution most favored by many — who did not give themselves the trouble to enquire of the highly respectable witnesses — was that of 'trickery by professional mediums from interested motives'. But such explanation entirely left out of account the fact that Mrs. Guppy, the real principal in the matter, is not a professional medium at all, and by social position is removed far above the operation of any such motive. Moreover Mrs. Guppy had, and has a reputation as a medium which is of European extent and includes the testimony of hundreds of persons of unimpeachable integrity in the best English and Continental society — society which would not continue to receive anyone addicted to purposed deception. Whatever the 'professional medium' solution may be worth it will not avail however as explaining Mr. Blank's 'transference', for none of the parties to the seance at Highbury, or witnesses at Kingsdown Road are professional mediums in any sense — while Mr. Blank not only makes no pretension to mediumship, so called, but is notorious amongst his friends as a great sceptic concerning the phenomena so frequently alleged to be of spiritual origin.

"It is worthy of notice in this connection that the evidence as to the 'departure' of Mrs. Guppy on her aerial flight was considered weak — at any rate numerically — it comprising beyond her own statement the testimony of Mr. Guppy and Miss Neyland only. But in the case of Mr. Blank the fact of 'departure' is a matter testified by nine witnesses besides himself. As a feature of likeness however between the two events we have in each case the fact of so-called mediumship, in some form or other, as present at both the 'departure' and 'arrival' points of the journeys.

"The theory that Mr. Blank himself played a practical joke, and duped several long-known friends, will doubtless be raised by many of your readers. We therefore urge attention to such further particulars as will aid those whose minds take that direction. First then on any theory of deception by Mr. Blank (and apart from his emphatic disclaimer of trickery) we would assert his absolute necessity for accomplices both inside and outside of the room as indispensable to the successful performance of such a conjuring feat. For in an incredibly short space of time he must have eluded the adjoining sitters, have got out of the totally dark room without allowing a ray of light to enter, have relocked the door, leaving the key in the lock upon the inside, and have replaced the cloth inside at the foot of the door. So far, however, as accomplices inside of the room are concerned, we for ourselves entirely reject that explanation. All the sitters in question are well-known to each other and to Mr. Blank and have frequently sat in seance before, together and with other visitors, we are thoroughly assured of each other's good faith, and can answer the one for the other — and for Mrs. Blank — as not having during the sitting for a moment quitted the table, which was nine or ten feet from the door. In regard to the outside of the room we have the testimony of Mrs. Guppy's servants, *immediately* sought and obtained, that they knew nothing whatever of the matter and had no cognizance of the fact, mode, or manner of Mr. Blank's departure from the house. The only other persons known to be in the house were the baby and a child but four years old, at that time in bed. Beyond this we are unable to venture any assertion as to outside accomplices (if any) and therefore put forward the fact of 'time' as of the most importance, apart from Mr. Blank's repeated assertion of his absolute unconsciousness of his transit.

"On the question of 'time' it must be borne in mind that the clocks and watches of private houses and individuals are not regulated with railway accuracy, and that we did not foresee or immediately realize that 'time' would be an element of so much importance in the seance. But it is remarkable that Mr. Stokes makes the arrival of Mr. Blank at Kingsdown Road to be about five minutes earlier than our estimated time of his departure from Highbury. Such a discrepancy, while easily accounted for as a difference between watches, *minimises* rather than otherwise, the interval necessary to Mr. Blank for his performance of the distance either by horse, cab, or running. In any case, the haste necessary to such a performance, in face of the sloppy road and wet weather of that night, must have left some traces of dirt. But such traces, on the testimony of Mr. Stokes and family, were not to be found on Mr. Blank, his boots especially being free from other than dry mud and only damp on the under part of the soles — a circumstance of considerable importance taken in connection with the distance of Moreland Villas from the cab thoroughfare; while the use of a vehicle at all is difficult to reconcile with the fact of perspiration on Mr. Blank's face; and further the seance itself being unpremeditated well nigh excludes the probability of that previous preparation obviously necessary on the part of Mr. Blank for the successful performance of a practical joke involving so much elaboration and such rapid exertion.

"But all those (and they are many) who like ourselves have the pleasure of Mr. Blank's acquaintance know him to be uncompromising in his endeavours to expose imposture. Indeed there is no more interesting feature of this case than that the 'transference' now recorded is not that of an acknowledged or alleged medium, as in former instances, but has occurred to a gentleman making no mediumistic claims and avowedly sceptical concerning the manifestations alleged to take place at seances. We cannot therefore (for ourselves) entertain the theory of 'practical joking by Mr. Blank' without attributing to him an untruthfulness of which we sincerely believe him incapable; to say nothing of the hospitality abused and the bad taste involved. And in this case it must be remembered that Mr. Blank was not dealing directly with 'Spiritualism' nor with thick and thin partisans thereof, but with several friends who own no higher relation to the subject than that of investigators, and who are entitled, as much as he is, to that social, professional and mercantile consideration he claims for himself. (Vide third paragraph.)

"It will occur to many that this event is not one of mere 'weight-carrying' but involves the passing of solid matter through solid matter, thus further complicating the case in favor of scepticism. To this we reply that however incredible the fact of solid matter passing through solid matter may appear, to persons who have not investigated the phenomena in question, it is none the less one of the best attested and, for years past, one of the most frequently occurring manifestations in the mediumship of Mrs. Guppy. As illustrating this feature of the case we are permitted to add for the further bewilderment of your readers that within the last months two other very remarkable seances have taken place at which some of us were present.

"At the first of these one of the undersigned visitors asked for a sunflower – a momentary wish on his part and one he certainly had not previously disclosed. Almost immediately a whole sunflower plant over six feet high was placed on the table together with half a bushel of mould about its roots. At the second sitting some forty articles were brought, including (among fruit, flowers and vegetables) two living goldfish, a live lobster and two live eels – one of which to the no small alarm and annoyance of Mrs. Guppy was placed around her neck. On both occasions the party sat under test conditions, and door and windows fastened and *all* present holding hands. The difference between bringing a sunflower plant into a closed and bolted room, and taking our Mr. Blank – a gentleman of over fifteen stone weight – is little more than that of degree and equally needs the explanation which we hope some of your intelligent readers may be able to afford.

"We are yours truly,

> P. Greck, 56 Hereford Road, Bayswater
> Felix Proszynszki, 56 Hereford Road, Bayswater
> William Volckmann, 12 King Edward Road, N.E.
> Margaret Fisher, 155 Palmer Terrace, Holloway Road
> Edward Fisher, 155 Palmer Terrace, Holloway Road
> Arthur Larkam, 32 Tolling Road
> Samuel Guppy, 1 Morland Villas, Highbury Hill Park
> Elizabeth Guppy, 1 Morland Villas, Highbury Hill Park

"P.S.: This record has been read by Mr. and Mrs. Blank and is forwarded for publication with their full cognisance."

One cannot question the honesty of this report. Mr. Blank, alias A. L. Henderson, could have conceivably tricked his friends. If so, he never came out with an exposure. On the contrary, a confirmation is quoted by Robert Cooper in *Light,* December 14, 1895, as follows:

> It was afterwards rumoured that Mr. Henderson had in some way played a trick, but on his calling one day at the offices of *The Spiritual Times* and being questioned on the subject, he maintained the truth of the occurrence which he said was a mystery to him.

The remarkable thing in all these transportation stories is that while those who had not witnessed them frequently expressed scepticism, not once did any witness raise an accusation of fraud or suggest a method by which the feat could have been normally accomplished.

A trap door on the ceiling at 61, Lamb's Conduit Street would not have been sufficient. Block and tackle would have been additionally needed, but no evidence of machinery ever was found in the upstairs-downstairs, hide-and-seek game of Messrs. Herne and Williams. The discovery of the same mediums in fraudulent production of different type of phenomena does not affect the case of transportation. Sooner or later, all mediums are discovered in fraud. Not because they always were fraudulent but because constant mediumistic practice often has a debilitating and demoralizing effect. Most mediums half of the time, trance mediums most of the time, do not know what they are doing. They are in mental states beyond conscious control. The average man shies from an ordinary hypnotic experiment for fear of surrendering his consciousness. These people deliberately enter into a state of amnesia and entrust their fate to nebulous entities that call themselves spirits (one of them a self-styled blood-thirsty pirate) and claim to be activated by the highest motives of serving humanity. Whether the trust is foolish or heroic, the measure of the failure of King & Co. in their mission argues more for an earthly effort emanating from the medium's unconscious, than for a supernatural one.

On behalf of the heroic description it should be stated that the physical phenomena of mediumship are known to impose a heavy strain on both body and mind. After a number of years, most physical mediums develop a strong craving for stimulants against constant nervous depletion, and end up as chronic alcoholics.* Physical and moral decline go together. It is much easier to produce seance room phenomena along the line of least resistance by normal means than by the expenditure of considerable psychic energy. As long as we know so little

*Stainton Moses, Henry Slade and Margery are outstanding examples.

about the psychology and physiology of this type of mediumship, it behooves us not to be hasty in our judgment.

◄ CHAPTER XVI ►

The Marquis Vanishes

When, in *Alice in Wonderland,* the Cheshire cat vanished, it left a grin. When a man vanishes, to appear mysteriously elsewhere in the same moment, the grin, sardonic, is on the face of the listener to the story. Who could blame him? It is a story that almost no amount of evidence, except repeated personal experience, could make believable.

The testimony of the man who disappeared would count the least. He would be accused of willful deception or of being mad. Utterly bewildered, he himself would incline to the latter explanation. Not until somebody reassured him that such things have been known to happen to others in history, would he feel ready to discuss the experience.

Those who indulge in spiritualistic practices, rightly or wrongly, have the advantage of such an assurance; even so it is by no means certain that they will not come to grief and regret the publication of such a mental-spacial adventure.

A case in point is that of the Marquis Carlo Centurione Scotto, Principe del Sacro Romano Impero, Conte di Visone, Marchese di Morzasco, Marchese di Castelnuove Scrivia, Principe di Goreto, etc., a Doctor of Law and Member of Parliament from 1909-20 in Rome. His high titles, the standing of his family, his personal reputation did not in the least make the adventure that befell him less preposterous.

It began with the death of his son, the Marquis Vittorio del Principi Centurione, a captain of the Italian Air Corps who, while flying over Lake Varese in order to test a new plane for entry into the American Schneider Cup race, was killed. This happened on September 21, 1926. The grief-stricken father was advised to seek comfort in reading an English book, Dennis Bradley's *Toward the Stars,* which was translated into Italian.

The book unfolds a remarkable story of the author's researches into Spiritualism through the means of his own mediumship which suddenly developed. Bradley, a writer of some reputation, told his story so impressively that the Marquis decided to pay him a visit in London and seek contact, in his circle, with his lost son. Ernesto Bozzano, the dean of Italian psychical researchers, provided him with a letter of introduction.

Luck was with the Marquis. George Valiantine, the American direct voice medium, at the time on the peak of his fame, was Bradley's guest and we are told that in the seance, which was thus doubly reinforced, the Marquis' son spoke to him in a voice that he recognized, and gave him evidence of his survival of death. In the very first seance, the sound of an aeroplane engine issued from the trumpet, then the sound of a fall, an imitation of Vittorio's tragic death of which — we are assured — neither Bradley nor Valiantine were informed.

The London seances over, Valiantine presented the Marquis with an aluminum trumpet and begged him to sit for the direct voice in his own house. He said the Marquis would develop and thus be able to get his own evidence as Bradley did. Whether his suggestion helped to awaken latent psychic faculties or not, the Marquis obtained from the very first seance a rapid and marvelous success. A voice spoke from the trumpet, which appeared to float in the dark, and it claimed to be the voice of Cristo d'Angelo, one of Valiantine's guides who said he had been a Sicilian shepherd on earth.

The seances were held at Millesimo Castle, in the Marquis' ancestral home. He never used a cabinet and rarely went into trance as he had an aversion to it. The trumpet was coated with luminous paint, but the voice also was heard without it, usually issuing from a corner of the ceiling. We are told that three languages and five dialects, unknown to the medium, were spoken, the dialects being Piedmontese, Romagnolo, Neapolitan, Venetian and Sicilian. Apport phenomena also were frequent, but to obtain these, the presence of Mme. Fabienne Rossi was necessary. Apparently she had the specific mediumistic talent for this feature.

Remarkably, however, the dead son failed to communicate, which was, perhaps, fortunate as the Marquis was not interested in the scientific side of these experiments nor did he have any wish to make spiritualistic propaganda. The chief witness, Ernesto Bozzano, found it an extremely delicate matter to suggest test conditions, for such suggestions implied that the Marquis might be guilty of deliberately deceiving his guests.

The remarkable event in which we are mainly interested, took place on July 29, 1928. The Marquis' guests in the circle consisted of Mme. Fabienne Rossi, her husband Mr. Paolo Rossi, Mrs. Gwendolyn Kelley Hack, a visiting American, widow of a New York physician, Ernesto Bozzano, Marchioness Luisa Centurione Scotto, Signorina Maria Chiappini, Signors Arrigo Passini, Gino Gibelli and two attorneys-at-law, Tullio Castellani and Piero Bon.

According to Ernesto Bozzano's account in *Luce e Ombra,* September-October, 1928, attested by all the witnesses, "the light was extinguished at 10:45 p.m. During the playing of the first few bars of music, a violent blast of wind passed over the sitters. Others followed of extraordinary intensity. A heavy table covered with vases of flowers and knick-knacks, standing outside the circle, was dragged about with a great deal of noise. It stopped for a moment and then moved on again, making a lot of noise. The table was completely outside the circle, yet it was displaced, and we discussed this as being an unusual circumstance. While the second record was being played the trumpet rose with the evident intention of going around the circle to greet everyone, but having reached the height of about six feet it stopped in the air, then the orifice slowly turned toward each person's face, almost as though it wished to scrutinize them."

After some conversation between the control, "Cristo d'Angelo," and the sitters:

"Mme. la Marquise Luisa noticed the presence of an entity between herself and M. Rossi. Muffled raps resounded from all parts of the room.

"M. Rossi stated that there had been a movement of the medium in his direction. He had the impression that he was near to him, and therefore he asked the Marquis whether he was still in his place. The medium replied that he was still in his chair, and that he had not moved at all. After a short pause M. Rossi had the same impression, and again asked the medium whether he had moved? The medium replied in the negative, and to prove that he was still in the same place he put out his hand to touch Mme. Fabienne Rossi, who was sitting on his right. He also did so in order to convince himself that he was not the victim of a strange illusion. Suddenly he exclaimed in a frightened voice 'I can no longer feel my legs.'

"At that moment the gramophone stopped, and in the general anxiety caused by the medium's exclamation, no one thought of restarting it. An interval of death-like silence followed.

"Mme. Fabienne Rossi: 'I feel as though something extraordinary were happening. I feel around me an indefinable vacuum which is very alarming.'

"Feeling frightened, Mme. la Marquise Luisa cried in a loud voice: 'Carlo! Carlo!'

"No answer.

"M. Castellani: 'Hush, the medium has fallen into a trance. Keep quiet. Don't move . . . . . M. Carlo, M. Carlo!'

"No answer.

"M. Castellani (to Mme. Rossi): 'Stretch out your hand to feel what position the medium is in.'

"Mme. Rossi stretched out her hand, and exclaimed: 'He is not there!'

"M. Rossi: 'Let us look on the sofa.'

"He rose and felt along the sofa, but there was no one on it. In the short time which had elapsed from the moment in which the medium had exclaimed, 'I can no longer feel my legs', until we noticed his disappearance, we did not hear the slightest sound in the room, no rustling of clothes, no sound of footsteps, no vibration of the floor, much less the sound of a key turning in the lock, or the door opening and re-shutting. The sitters began to feel terribly alarmed and agitated.

"M. Castellani: 'We must be very calm. Everything depends upon Mme. la Marquise, who must show her strength of character. No harm can happen to the medium.' (Addressing Cristo d'Angelo) 'You see what a state we are in. You must tell us where the medium is. On you alone rests the peace of our mind.'

"We waited anxiously but in vain, for Cristo d'Angelo to reply.

"M. Bozzano: 'It is quite useless to expect Cristo d' Angelo to answer us; in the absence of his medium he cannot speak.'

"We discussed the advisability of lighting the red lamp.

"M. Bozzano: 'We are confronted by the phenomenon of the asportation or the transportation of the medium. A phenomenon which has occurred on former occasions. Therefore, the red lamp can be lit without fear.'

"The red light was turned on, but the medium was not in the room. The doors were still securely locked, with the key on the inside of the door, but the medium had disappeared. We searched for him in the adjacent rooms, but found no one. It was suggested that we should have a table seance, and this was tried, but the answers were vague and contradictory. One might almost have thought that they did not wish the medium to be disturbed during this period of restorative sleep, but we did not think of this explanation until after the solution of the mystery. At this moment a terrible anxiety tormented us all.

"With great caution M. Castellani and M. Passini searched all the rooms of the castle, but their return only increased our alarm, for they found no one, absolutely no one. M. Castellani remarked that according to the law of psychic rapport the medium would no doubt be discovered in a place which would be in sympathy with his tastes and interests, and sure enough it was in such a place that he was found. Mme. la Marquise, therefore, suggested that we ought to search the stables, on account of her husband's passion for horses. M. Castellani and M. Passini rushed to the stables and searched all the horse-boxes and all the carriages but their search was in vain.

"Following a suggestion we had obtained by means of raps, we returned to the medium's own room, but found no one there. Then we all congregated in the seance room, and sat in a circle holding hands; we persevered in this for twenty minutes without obtaining anything but some currents of air. M. Bozzano said he thought it was quite useless to continue, because the supernormal return of anyone 'asported' in this way has never been recorded, and therefore it was necessary for us to continue the hunt until we found the Marquis. Meanwhile two and a half hours had passed in our vain search of the castle. The cellars, the stables, the family chapel, and even the grounds had been explored.

"Mme. la Marquise prepared to send a car to Genoa in the hope of finding her husband in their palace in Via Caffaro. M. Castellani and M. Gibelli offered to start immediately, but before taking such a drastic step M. Rossi and M. Passini proposed that Mrs. Hack — who is gifted with fine writing mediumship — should try to get into communication with her spirit Guide "Imperator", for information. About 1:00 A.M., Mrs. Hack acceding to their request, asked the help of her guides, who immediately communicated by means of automatic writing. Addressing Mme. la Marquise, they wrote in Italian:

" 'Do not be anxious, we are watching and guarding.'

"They persistently declared that the Marquis was lying prone on something and kept repeating the word 'asleep, asleep'. They added that when found M. Castellani would know how to awake him. (This proved to be a sort of prediction, for that is what eventually happened.) Some time later Mrs. Hack made a second attempt to get into communication with her Guide, 'Imperator'. First the profile of a face was drawn and 'White Eagle' was written (the symbol and name of her Red Indian Guide) followed by three rough crosses, which is the sign that her Guide 'Imperator', is present. He wrote as follows:

" 'Carry one thought and ask. (Pause) The medium sleeps but you will have some more searching to do before you find him. (Pause)'

"Mrs. Hack: 'Where is he?'

'He is not in Genoa. He is on the premises but remote. He is on the premises but sleeps.'

"Mrs. Hack: 'But where?'

'Go to the right, then outside. Wall and Gate. He is lying—hay—hay— on a soft place.' + (Imperator's Sign) 'Try to go and look.' (To M. Rossi) 'Be careful of the servants and beware of an alarm. We are going to direct you. Take Fabienne and his coat.'

"M. Passini, Mino, M. Castellani and Mlle. Chiappini ran towards the granary indicated, which was in the stable yard. When they reached the entrance to the stables they found that the great entrance door was locked, and that the key was not in the lock. Mino and Mme. Chiappini ran to fetch it, for it was kept on a nail in the outer entrance of the stables. We entered, feeling our way in the pitch darkness, not taking a light because we had been specially warned not to wake anyone. Suddenly Mino stopped, saying under his breath that he heard somebody snoring in the granary. The reader will remember that 'Imperator' had mentioned that the medium would be found fast asleep in the hay.

"We were all overjoyed. Mino switched on an electric torch which gave but a feeble light, and we saw a small door which had previously been overlooked. This door was locked, the key being in the keyhole on the outside of the door. We opened it with the greatest caution, and we immediately saw two well-shod feet pointing towards the door. The light was extinguished, and M. Castellani entered the granary with M. Passini.

"On a heap of hay and oats the medium was comfortably lying, immersed in profound sleep. M. Castellani made a few magnetic passes over the Marquis, and almost immediately he commenced to move, groaning pitifully. When he first began to regain consciousness and found himself lying in the stable on the hay and oats, with M. Passini and M. Castellani near him, he completely lost his bearings, feared that he had gone out of his mind and burst into tears. M. Castellani tried to calm him, telling him that the reason why they were in this granary was because on the preceding evening they had drunk too heavily, and that they had fallen asleep in the hay.

"The medium was amazed. Then he exclaimed that this could never have happened, that he must be the victim of a practical joke, and that it was too bad to treat him so. He began to call loudly for his wife and son. His son immediately ran up, followed by Mme. Luisa. At the sight of his dear ones he brightened up and became calmer, agreeing to await a more opportune moment for the recital of what had actually taken place. When we reached the verandah, on our return, it was three o'clock in the morning. The phenomenon of the disappearance and 'asportation' of the medium occurred at 11:30 P.M.

"The above description of the phenomenon of the 'asportation' of the medium from a securely locked room seems to me to be sufficient not to need any further explanation. I will but add that in order to reach the granary one must leave the castle, and walk a distance of 60 metres (over 60 yards) through the grounds. In order to deposit the medium in the granary on the hay and oats it was necessary to pass through four locked doors: namely, the door of the seance room, the entrance door of the castle, the large entrance of the stable, and the small door of the granary. How did the medium get there? How was it done? That the little door of the granary was locked, and that the key was in the lock on the outside, absolutely precludes the possibility of the medium accomplishing his own translocation by normal means or while in a somnambulistic state.

"It will be noticed that during the very short period which elapsed between the time when the medium exclaimed: 'I can no longer feel my legs', and his disappearance, absolute silence reigned in the room, so that it would have been impossible for him to make any movement without being heard; while the grating of the key turning in the lock, or the sound of the door being opened and shut would have been still more plainly audible. This does not take into account that were the medium walking in his sleep, when once he had passed through the door it would have been impossible for him to shut it behind him, and leave the key in the lock on the inside of the door. It is therefore utterly useless to advance the theory that the medium walked out of the seance room while in a somnambulistic state. This theory cannot stand, for it is opposed by the facts.

"Another circumstance is very interesting, namely, that in order to perform this 'asportation' or 'translation' of the medium and for the searchers to find the keys in the locks, as we did, it would require two persons to be in collusion. In which case, the somnambulistic hypothesis would fall to the ground, but another theory might be advanced in its stead, namely that of a pseudo-medium who for the sake of amusement, and in order to create fictitious evidence of pseudo-supernormal power, had secured an 'accomplice' to assist him by shutting him up in the granary, leaving the key in the lock on the outside. But on this theory it is necessary that the 'accomplice' be one of our group of sitters, for he must be in the seance room at the beginning of the experiment ready to relock the door on the inner side after the medium had slipped out leaving the key in the lock; and this he must accomplish without the other sitters hearing any movement or being aware of anyone passing between one chair and another, in the circle (the chairs only being separated by a distance of about eight inches) and without our hearing the key being turned in the lock of the door, or the sound of a door being opened and shut. Then the 'accomplice', after having followed the pseudo-medium as far as the granary, would have to lock him in, and then return to the seance room unobserved. This he would certainly not succeed in doing, because directly the absence of the medium was discovered we turned on the red light in the seance room, and when the little red lamp was lighted not one of the sitters was missing.

"It is, therefore, useless to consider such vain and absurd theories. For the somnambulistic hypothesis, and that of 'accomplices' will not stand the analysis of the facts, and one is forced to concede that we are confronted by the authentic phenomenon of the 'asportation' or the 'transportation' of a living person. I realize that such a phenomenon must appear so monstrous and incredible, that the majority of my readers, not having been present themselves, will be unable to admit its possibility. All we can do in reply to these waverers is to quote one of Professor Richet's sayings: 'Yes, you are quite right, we are describing an impossible phenomenon; and yet it is true!' In other words, facts are facts, and it is quite vain and unscientific to contest them, for our rudimentary senses cannot penetrate the mystery of existence."

Bozzano was committed to the dematerialization theory. He thought that the dematerialization of the Marquis' body commenced at the time of his report that he no longer could feel his legs. The conclusion is totally unwarranted. The sensation of partial anesthesia reported by the Marquis may have been part of his impending entrancement which appears to be an indispensable preliminary to transportation.

Why, despite the reported presence of several spirit guides, did over two and a half hours pass in the search for the Marquis? According to Bozzano:

"We all agreed that the reason why our spirit Guides obstinately refused to inform us for so long as so where they had hidden the medium, could probably be explained by their determination to prevent our disturbing the Marquis during the long period of sleep which was necessary to restore his vital forces, following such a great output of energy. As already stated, 'Imperator', the spirit Guide, when he revealed the whereabouts of the medium, added, 'The medium sleeps, but you will have some more searching to do before you find him . . . . He is lying . . . hay . . . hay. Try to go and look,' which shows that it would have been imprudent to disturb him any sooner.

"In order that he should not be found before the necessary time had elapsed which would enable him to regain his strength, it was necessary to conceal him so successfully, as to prevent twelve persons from finding him; and this reveals the great perspicacity of the operating spirit personalities for it would have been impossible to find a more secure hiding place in the whole castle and grounds than the one which they chose. Evidently we were intended to overlook that small white door set in a white wall, during our nocturnal search, lighted only by the feeble flame of a candle; and it quite escaped our notice, as it was meant to do, so that there should be no risk to the medium's health through his being awakened during the early phases of his trance.

"We must never forget that it was Mrs. Hack, who, by means of automatic writing, relieved our terrible anxiety, and through her mediumship was able to direct us to the hiding place where we found the Marquis sleeping peacefully. We should not overlook the supernormal source from whence we received this important information. Mrs. Gwendolyn Hack, a distinguished American lady, was making a short stay in Genoa, and was invited to take part in our sittings. She was totally unfamiliar with the outbuildings surrounding the ancient castle of Millesimo, and above all she had no idea as to where the stables were situated. She writes to me as follows:

> 'With regard to the information furnished by my guide, "Imperator", whose instructions led to the immediate finding of the medium, I must point out a very important truth: that I had no knowledge of the locality described in which the Marquis would shortly be found. It was absolutely impossible for such information – which was written without the slightest hesitation – to have come from my brain or from my subconscious mind. I had never been on that side of the castle, and had

> neither seen nor entered the stables, which were on a lower level than that of the castle. Therefore, these instructions must, of necessity, have come from a source outside my personal knowledge, conscious or subconscious.' "

The story as told by Bozzano is based on the notes of Mrs. Hack, from which a statement was drawn up and signed by all the witnesses the following day. Another individual record was made not more than eight hours after the Marquis' disappearance by Signorina Maria Chiappini. The agreement regarding all the essential facts is complete.

However, something else, from an outside source, has been claimed as part of the body of the evidence. "Cristo d'Angelo" was not the only spirit borrowed by the Marquis from Valiantine. The presence of another, called "Bert Everett," also was announced on the night of the transportation.

Paolo Rossi, having gone on a visit to London, entered into correspondence with Valiantine, now back in New York, and requested him to ask "Bert Everett" whether he could describe a notable manifestation in which he had taken part at Millesimo Castle. In a letter dated October 23, 1928, Valiantine quoted "Bert Everett" as saying that he was at Millesimo Castle a great many times with Cristo d'Angelo, was present when the Marquis was "apported" in the barn and helped at the time.

Ernesto Bozzano considered this claim from New York "as a wonderful corroboration of the authenticity of the facts, and also as a proof of the independence of Bert Everett as a spirit entity." He points out that his report of the Marquis' transportation, in the September-October, 1928, issue of *Luce e Ombra,* was published late and did not appear until the beginning of November.

His enthusiasm is deplorable. It is impossible that Paolo Rossi would have preserved discreet silence over the exciting events at Millesimo Castle while he was in London. He wrote to Valiantine twice, once on September 15, the second time on October 5. There was plenty of time until October 23 for Valiantine to hear of a story that must have spread like wildfire among the London spiritualists.

During the evening of the day following the Marquis' transportation, Mrs. Hack made notes of the Marquis' impressions and recollections from his dictation. As quoted by Mrs. Hack, prior to the seance,

> the Marquis had felt fresh and calm, being genial in his conversation and in good spirit all the afternoon and during and after dinner. The sitters were given no intimation that anything momentous was about to occur. The hour was late, conversation through the direct voice had been going on for some time and they expected an early finish. Cristo d'Angelo actually announced that the force for the voice is beginning to wane but there is still force for one materialisation. It was after this announcement that the position of the Marquis was queried. He gave his impressions the following day as follows:
>
> At this instant I could not feel my legs any more, having the impression of going into trance. I asked Fabienne (Rossi) for her hand, which I took really willingly to reassure myself. After having taken the hand I felt something descend over my brain and my face – and I felt myself light . . . light . . . light . . . but of such lightness! (motions with arms as if of wings) . . . . I felt myself as if fainting, and I . . . Then I recall nothing more. Nothing – nothing.

The Marquis weighed approximately 190 pounds and was a tall man, extremely athletic in build and as guides in London sittings described him, "of exceptional vitality." He was fully dressed, wearing shoes of ordinary heaviness. Upon being found he was dressed just as before.

Of his feelings on awakening on the hay in the barn the Marquis stated:

> The first moment when I awakened was a most sorrowful moment and I seemed to be in another world. I was not afraid, but felt – supernormal. Then, following upon my awakening, to assure myself that I was in this world and not in another, I at once called my son and wife. I saw near to me my son, and I realised that I was here. And next I thought "they have brought me here as a joke, etc.," in seeing myself surrounded by various persons.

Mino Centurione, the son, arrived at one o'clock at night, during the fruitless search for his father. It is not stated from where he came or who vouched for his arrival. The question is one of the many which arise when the wise owls of psychical research step in and try to tear Bozzano's story to pieces on the premise that it is easier to stretch the intent to deceive to the utmost than to admit something as stupendous as Bozzano's claim.

◂ CHAPTER XVII ▸

The Marquis Retreats

THE CRITICS of mediumistic phenomena pounced like wolves on Bozzano's report of the Marquis Centurione Scotto's transportation. It is at least an excellent intellectual exercise to follow in their footsteps and to see how willingly they will drag everybody into the mud for the sake of preserving vested scientific interests.

The offensive was begun by Dr. Rudolph Lambert in the August, 1929, issue of the Berlin *Zeitschrift für Parapsychologie.* He first points out that

> the chief mediums, the Marquis and Mrs. Rossi seem to be sitting generally side-by-side, at any rate, this seems to be the case on the occasion of the disappearance of the Marquis. Mrs. Rossi sat on the right of the medium, on the left stood the table with the gramophone, so that of all of the participants in the sitting the Marquis possessed the greatest freedom of movements.

He further objects that Bozzano never gives the order of the sitters. "That he gives no plan of the sitting room, that we do not even learn how many doors the room had. It is only from a casual remark that we can infer that it was a communicating room, therefore it had at least two doors. It is worthy of note that on the wish of the Marchioness the sitting room was changed to an isolated room, but the control insisted on the previous one; it is not impossible, therefore, that the Marquis, for the purpose of enlisting the help of an assistant, had preference for a room with several doors. Bozzano was so convinced that he was witnessing genuine phenomena that he forgot to note as trifles such possibilities.

"The great event begins with a statement of the Marchioness that there is someone between her and Rossi. Knocks were heard from every direction. If the observation of the Marchioness was correct, this being could have been the Marquis engaged in opening the door and at the same time knocking in various directions on the wall in which his big figure could have been helpful. Mr. Rossi then remarked that the Marquis was near him. His impression was so definite that he asked the Marquis if he was in his place, whereupon the Marquis answered, yes, and he did not move. After a short interval Mr. Rossi had the same impression once again, and asked the Marquis if he was still in his seat. He affirmed and as a proof he put out his hand towards Mrs. Rossi on his right. He does so to convince himself that he is not labouring under an illusion of his senses. Then he cries: 'I do not feel my legs'. As at the same time the gramophone stops, and in the general excitement no one thought of starting it again, a period of great silence ensued; this was followed by excited talking on the part of several people. Castellani spoke to d'Angelo and received no answer. This would have been natural if the direct voice was produced through the instrumentality of the Marquis and he was no more in the room.

"We see that Bozzano thinks immediately of a highly occult phenomenon without first exhausting normal possibilities. It is stated (by whom?) that the doors are shut and the key is in the keyhole. There is a search for some hours in the castle and in the stables as, owing to the Marquis' fondness of horses, they think it possible as the place of transportation. Finally they ask Mrs. Hack, who is an automatic writer, to consult her control, Imperator. The answer came that the Marquis was in deep sleep, they should go out, then turn right, you will find a little door in the wall, there he lies in a soft spot, hay. . .hay. . .hay. It is said that these instructions were correct. Acting on them, Mino, the Marquis' son who did not take part in the sitting, Castellani and Passini found him in the place indicated, the door leading there being locked, the key on the outside.

"At the beginning of his report Bozzano forgets to say whether the door of the seance room was locked. Let us suppose that this was the case. Bozzano believes that after the cry of the Marquis, 'I can no longer feel my legs', there was such a silence that every movement of the Marquis would have been observed, especially the grating of the key in the keyhole and the noise of the opening and closing of the door. Further, the Marquis could not have closed the door from the inside after he was out of it. In the place where he was discovered the key was similarly on the outside, so Bozzano wisely thinks that the feat could not have been performed by fraud without help. Moreover, according to Bozzano, a member of the circle would have had to accompany him to lock him in, then he would have had to return for which there was no sufficient time as the red light was put on and the circle was found complete. From this Bozzano infers that the case of transportation was genuine. I confess I am not convinced. The events could be construed in this light:

"The suspicious movements of the Marquis before his disappearance were for the purpose of opening the door. The Marquis then only had to walk out and hide himself. While people were looking for him in anxiety the same helper who brought the big apports to the door, locked him in the stable. Of course, there was need of further assistance in the seance room. The assistant had to turn the key in the door through which the Marquis disappeared before the examination commenced; isn't it possible to think that Mrs. Rossi or the Marchioness could have done it in the general excitement which followed? It could have taken place in the moment when the lady in question verified if the door was locked.

"Therefore, it is regrettable that Bozzano omits to say who examined the door after the light was put on. With this I do not mean to say that during the anxious search in the darkness there was no opportunity to do it; Bozzano, immediately on suspecting the disappearance of the Marquis, should have personally examined the door. It is not the fault of those who criticize his report that he did not do so. When Bozzano says that the Marquis, even with the help of an assistant, could not have left the room unobserved, because only a distance of about 20 centimeters separated the sitters, he forgets his own statement that the space between the Marquis and Mr. Rossi was bigger. The gramophone table stood between them, so that the Marquis had the greatest freedom of motion, having at the same time on his other side Mrs. Rossi, the other medium. Also, after the disappearance, his neighbours, the two Rossis, were fairly free to move. There is the suspicious circumstance to which Mr. Rossi twice called attention, the nearness of the Marquis to him; he may have wanted more room by pushing the table. Bozzano explains that in the place between Mr. Rossi and the Marquis a condensation of the dematerialised body of the Marquis was taking place. This is how a circumstance of suspicion becomes an interesting occult phenomenon.

"If the automatic script of Mrs. Hack on the whereabouts of the medium is not a chance hit, or if it was not inspired by a hint from an accomplice within the circle, this message, at least, would be an occult phenomenon, demonstrating a telepathic rapport between the Marquis and Mrs. Hack. But even if this lady had proved something unquestionably occult it would not yet follow that the phenomena at Millesimo Castle were genuine.

"Undoubtedly, the hypothesis here advanced is improbable as it requires the cooperation of three people (except if the key in the lock could have been turned from the inside), presumably above suspicion, to perpetrate an infamous fraud. But considering that there was no proper control the hypothesis of Bozzano is still more improbable, namely that spirits (who were unable, as we have seen, to get in touch with the members of the circle in the room, once the sitting was broken) have disintegrated the body of the Marquis and have taken him through several locked doors to another place where they recondensed it. Such explanation should only be drawn into consideration when no normal solution is left; for this purpose the phenomenon should be observed under the strongest possible control in several circles. The more preposterous and rare the phenomenon is the more we should prefer a natural explanation as the one advanced. No researchers should acknowledge such extraordinary phenomena on the basis of a single, very unsatisfactorily controlled observation."

To this criticism Signor Bozzano returned* the following answer:

> It remains yet to discuss the asportation of the medium but I give it up for I find the methods of my critic revolting; they are methods against which earnest and well-balanced people must rise in protest. How can you discuss anything with an adversary who is fully determined to avail himself of an endless chain of infamous insinuations or vapid suppositions which he combines with a total absence of scruples? He piles suspects upon suspects against all. For instance, as regards the door which was found duly locked with the key on the inside, my adversary observes: "Isn't is possible to think that Mrs. Rossi or the Marchioness have done it in the general excitement which followed? It could have taken place in the moment when the lady in question verified if the door was locked." With that he intends not to affirm that the fact was verified since he is well aware that the two gentlemen did not claim to have made the verification. It is only an opportunity to advance an insinuation and get away with it. It follows, therefore, that the two ladies are suspected of complicity. After this I only want to observe that his long criticism is founded throughout on similar wrong presumptions and unscrupulous accusations into which also the servant girl is dragged in, who, on her part, is busily engaged in helping the enterprise to a good finish. To what indignity the criticism stoops is clearly visible from this statement:
>
> "Undoubtedly, the hypothesis here advanced is improbable as it requires the co-operation of three people, presumably above suspicion, to perpetrate an infamous fraud. But considering that there was no proper control, the hypothesis of Bozzano is still more improbable."
>
> In view of his recognition of what his own hypothesis is worth, I naturally take the attitude that its discussion would be equivalent to minimizing my personal dignity; so I limit myself to the declaration that, also in the name of my colleagues

**Luce e Ombra,* September 1929, pp. 398-99.

> in the group, I repudiate with contempt the insensate calumnies of an ignoramus.

In *Luce e Ombra,* February, 1930, (quoted in *Psychic Science,* 1930, p. 141) Bozzano further states:

> He commences by accusing the principal medium of continuous fraud, regardless of the fact that the experience took place in the intellectual surroundings of a family of the oldest nobility, and without taking into consideration that the tragic death of the medium's adored eldest son, killed three months previously, was the principal cause of the experiences, which had been started on the suggestion of a friend in the hope of being able to communicate with his spirit. The Marquis Centurione had never previously taken any interest in metapsychical investigations. The incidents are undoubtedly of the greatest importance in proving the genuineness of the facts, and combined with the numerous manifestations that are literally impossible to produce by fraud, should dissipate all doubt as to the truth of the phenomena. Professor Lambert, however, evaded and passed by imperturbably the pathetic psychological impulse which gave rise to the Millesimo experiences, attempting to explain everything on the supposition of the medium's fraud. However, he soon perceived that the manifestations were frequently so complex, and on such a large scale, that they could not be explained by the fraud of only one person, so he hastened to accuse the other medium of being an accomplice. He then recognized that he could not elucidate a great part of the phenomena by such an expedient, and therefore conceived "two comrades" listening at the doors, always in readiness to provide the medium with anything that he might require for the mystification of his friends, who conveniently slept like dormice and did not notice anything. Unfortunately for him, even with the help of this latest fable, he was unable to explain the numerous incidents in which the most private affairs of some of the sitters were mentioned. So he did not scruple to accuse the persons concerned of lying. He thus cruelly slanders four of the experimentalists, amongst whom were two distinguished gentlewomen. In spite of such audacity he may not be equal

> to explaining the facts, and then he may run to the extreme of declaring that he does not believe any of the circumstances related by me whenever they contain facts that cannot be explained by "fraud". And one cannot deny that any obstacle could be overcome in such manner. However, it had not occurred to him that his genial system of scientific criticism would demolish any series of metapsychical and scientific experiences if it were applied to them, naturally comprising those most remarkable experiences of his friend Professor Schrenck-Notzing. Also, that his triumph might become a personal disaster, for there is nothing to prevent me from imitating his system by declaring that I do not believe anything he has ever said, or may say, about his own experiences, past, present, or future, thus settling the account between us, but making use of a senseless, ridiculous basis, and a method of criticism anything but scientific.

Visibly, feelings were running at white heat over the Millesimo Mystery. Bozzano's indignation is commendable. He was present, he knew all the parties concerned, hence he had psychological data for his convictions which the mere critic cannot claim to possess as in none of these documents do we find a psychological portrait of the participants. But Lambert is also right on his own grounds. He need have had no sentimental considerations and as a self-constituted guardian of science he had to go to the utmost limits for the sake of preserving sanity. In some respects he did not even go far enough. He misses the point that the key being outside in the lock is not evidence, and the effect does not even necessitate an accomplice. Anyone can lock himself into a room if he has a plier to grab the end of the key protruding from the lock on the inside. The plier would not leave a mark on the key if a piece of paper were wrapped around the end before the grip is applied.

Following Lambert, Theodore Besterman continued

the attack in his review of Mrs. G. K. Hack's book, *Modern Psychic Mysteries at Millesimo Castle:*

> It cannot be disguised that Signor Bozzano's reports do not in themselves merit serious attention on evidential grounds. They show an almost complete lack of understanding of what constitutes good evidence and adequate recording of mediumistic sittings. Grounds for this accusation can be found on every page of his reports; but it is unnecessary to attempt a detailed criticism, the more so as this task had already been admirably performed (in regard to Signor Bozzano's original Italian reports) by Herr Lambert in the *Zeitscrift fur Parapsychologie* (1929 IV. 465-482). I am in full agreement with nearly all the remarks of Herr Lambert.

The following general observations are advanced by Mr. Besterman:

> These sittings were held (with a few unimportant exceptions) without any measure of control whatever, in complete darkness, with a gramophone playing practically all the time, in the Marquis Centurione Scotto's own home, in the presence of his family and friends, those present not being searched, the seating arrangement not being described (though it appears from certain incidents that the two mediums sat side by side) and in a room which is nowhere directly described. Indirect observations and two rough sketches (not to scale and apparently not parts of the original reports) show as that this room had doors on three of its sides and a window (opening apparently over a garden) on the fourth side.
>
> About the "apports" and "asports" he expresses the view that "the evidence for the supernormal nature of these phenomena is so slight that it requires a mental effort even to seriously criticize it.

Of the transportation of the Marquis he restricts himself to this sentence:

> Signor Bozzano proceeds to still further "conclusive" instances, such as the levitation of the Marquis with a chair and his "asportation" from the room;

> but it seems useless to continue our analysis. It must be already obvious that Signor Bozzano's claims are wholly unfounded, and that the Millesimo sittings have not the slightest vestige of scientific value.*

There was an unexpected emotional reaction to this criticism. Sir Arthur Conan Doyle resigned his membership in the Society for Psychical Research and, in a letter addressed to the Chairman of the Council, expressed himself in strong words:

> It is in my judgment, such a series of misrepresentations and insulting innuendos that it tends to lower the good name of the society. The insolence by which the considered opinion of a man like Professor Bozzano, who was present, is set aside and treated with contempt by one who was not present, and who has had very little experience of psychical research, makes one ashamed that such stuff should be issued by an official of a Society which has any scientific standing.

Conan Doyle was, of course, totally wrong. He was trying to make an emotional issue out of a scientific one. The review, he thought, implied the insinuation that an Italian nobleman of old family, a member of the legislative body, had invited a circle of friends to his home in order to practice a succession of complicated frauds upon them. That the Marquis himself was implicated is shown by the fact that levitation of his own body and other personal phenomena are among those most clearly recorded . . . .

> I have long waited hoping that the Podmore, Dingwall, Besterman tradition of obtuse negation at any cost would die away. But as there is no sign of it, and the obsession seems rather to become more pronounced, my only resource is, after thirty-six years of patience, to resign my own membership and to

**Journal, S.P.R.,* January, 1930, pp. 10-14.

> make some sort of public protest against the essentially unscientific and biassed work of a Society which has for a whole generation produced no constructive work of any kind, but has confined its energies to the misrepresentation and hindrance of those who have really worked at the most important problem ever presented to mankind.

This letter was enclosed in a circular letter which Conan Doyle sent to all the members of the S. P. R. In it he further said:

> This matter is of more importance than would at first sight appear, for I say deliberately that these Millesimo sittings are on the very highest possible level of psychical research, both from the point-of-view of accurate reporting, variety of phenomena, and purity of mediumship. Therefore, if they can be laughed out of court anything we can produce will be treated with similar contempt . . . . I have therefore resigned my membership, and the protest would be more effective if those who agree with me would see their way to follow my example.

Only six members accepted Conan Doyle's invitation to resign in protest. The outburst was unwarranted from the beginning as the review was signed by Besterman and rested on his own responsibility, which was never considered too heavy to upset equally or better qualified opinion. Conan Doyle gave him a build-up when he made him a virtual spokesman of the Society for Psychical Research. Intolerance is always regrettable from whatever camp it issues. In this case it has led to regrettable consequences. The Marquis refused to be the football between the Berlin Dodgers and the London Giants and denied all further permission of reports concerning his seances. I have a letter from Bozzano, dated April 26, 1934, in which he states:

> You are right in suspecting that the Marquis Centurione gave up psychical research because of the

> treatment he received at the hands of these gentlemen. It is so; nevertheless throughout these years I have attended some marvellous seances in his family circle, but I have been forbidden to publish aught about them.

Bozzano is now dead. Nobody seems to know what happened to the Marquis in later years. So much is evident; in a scientific age no one can play Cheshire cat with impunity. That the Marquis recognized it, is a credit to his intelligence. He was not motivated by the missionary spirit. He did not want to convince the world of human survival after death and of communication with the dead, nor of the reality of a psychic force. He was not interested in Spiritualism as a movement and he wanted nothing less than to be made a propagandist of the cause. He was just a plain father who was devoted to his son and was severely traumatized by his tragic death. He saw a way to annulling the loss through Spiritualism by establishing contact with the dead.

As long as he failed to get into contact with his son in his own seance room, he had to go on. The more marvellous the phenomena, the nearer he was to proving the existence of another state of life, of another dimension, with powers beyond earthly comprehension. His own transportation was, I believe, the culminating attempt to provide this evidence, not for others, but for himself. To be made a bone in a dog fight was unpleasant and distasteful, but it may have also sent a chill of apprehension through him. Whether voices are produced by some abnormal vocal development, whether objects are moved at a distance or drawn through space as if by magnetic action, the *spiritus rector* behind the phenomena is always the medium; and the mediums know it although the *modus operandi* escapes their understanding. We have no reason to assume that the Marquis felt differently. While science is totally unable to grapple with the fundamentals of mediumistic psychology, he who is not prepared to be a sacrificial victim must not be blamed for beating an early retreat.

◂ CHAPTER XVIII ▸

Spirits — or the Unconscious?

THE CASE presentation is now finished. We have reached the point where we must decide whether a genuine mystery is concealed behind ancient and modern records of transportation, or whether all is myth, illusion and fraud.

We have in the course of our inquiry considered various agencies from the Spirit of the Lord to the spirits of the dead. In having arrived at the spirits of the dead, however, we have not yet exhausted the list of possibilities. For when we peer beneath the surface of the evidence for spirits we find, astonishingly enough, that spirits may not be responsible at all — that, in fact, they may be only camouflage for the actual agency.

The ability displayed by the so-called spirit operators in engineering the feat of transportation appears beyond human power. What are these spirit operators? Are they, indeed, spirits of the dead?

The first observation one is prompted to make is that transportation by spirits never involves a departed relative. The personality who assumes responsibility for it always is a regular guide and more often than not a fantastic personality whose identity and life on earth cannot be established. That these spirit guides exist as autonomous personality organizations cannot be denied. But that does not bar the possibility that they are spirits in name only, in want of better designation and in consequence of suggestion by their audience and by their acceptance of such suggestion.

Unknown to himself (because he never applied it to the phenomena of the seance room) Jung has furnished the key to the real evaluation of these mysterious personalities. They are archetypes, not vague ideas grouped together in the unconscious under the guise of the Wise Man or the Mysterious Fellow Traveler, but actual projections of the archaic contents of the mediumistic mind, organized through its need and the need of its group into a guiding personality that, owing to its emergence from the inner sanctuary of the human psyche, is possessed of the ability to tap organismic energies in a manner not yet known to biologists.

The story of John King fits in with this view to perfection. I quote from the *Encyclopaedia of Psychic Science*:

"KING, JOHN, the most romantic spirit control. He claims to have been Henry Owen Morgan, the buccaneer, who was knighted by Charles II, and was appointed Governor of Jamaica. He first appeared with the Davenport Brothers in 1850 and was first seen in the flash of a pistol fired by Ira Davenport in the dark. He remained as spirit manager with the Davenports throughout their career and in typtology or direct voice gave them sound advice in difficult positions. His activity was multifarious. While faithfully serving the Davenport brothers he took charge of the performances in the Koon loghouse in the wilds of Ohio. Here he assumed an august mein. As the head of a band of 160 spirits he claimed descent from a race of men known by the generic term Adam and having as leaders "the most ancient angels." They signed their communications as

King No. 1, No. 2, etc., and sometimes: Servant and Scholar of God. In his last incarnation he strayed from the path of virtue and became a redoubtable pirate. He communicated in direct voice through a trumpet, his own invention, and through direct scripts. The tone of these writings was sanctimonious and upbraiding, i.e.: 'We know that our work will be rejected by many, and condemned as the production of their King Devil, whom they profess to repudiate, but do so constantly serve by crucifying the truth and rejecting all that is contrary to their own narrow pride and vain imaginings.'

"In the early years of English spiritualism it was the aspiration of many mediums to secure his influence. Mrs. Marshall was the first, Mrs. Guppy, Miss Georgina Houghton, Mrs. Firman, Williams, Eglinton and Husk followed, while in America he was claimed by the Holmeses and Mme. Blavatsky in her early career as a spiritualist. Solovyoff even suggests that Mahatma Koot Hoomi was John King transformed by the addition of an Eastern garb.

"The identity of John King with Henry Owen Morgan, the pirate, never has been satisfactorily established. Conan Doyle had in his possession a contemporary picture of the buccaneer king but it bore no resemblance to the tall, swarthy man with a noble head and full black beard who presented himself in materialized form. But he adds that a daughter of a recent governor of Jamaica was confronted in a seance in London with John King. He said to her: 'You have brought back from Jamaica something which was mine.' She asked: 'What was it?' He answered: 'My will.' It was a fact. Her father brought back this document.

"To Admiral Moore, in a sitting with Cecil Husk on March 28, 1905, John King said that he had been hunting up old records and found that he succeeded Lynch as Governor of Jamaica. There was a Richard Morgan who came before him as governor and the names sometimes were confused. He believes that he was governor three separate times – not consecutively – but he would make further inquiries.

"A correspondent to *Light* (June 29, 1912) looked up the official handbook of the island and found that he succeeded Sir Thomas Lynch in 1673, Lord Vaughn in 1677 and the Earl of Carlisle in 1680. The other Morgan to whom he referred was Colonel Edward (not Richard) Morgan and he was deputy governor in 1664."

This is an abbreviated account of John King's role in modern Spiritualism. The fantastic ideas with which he was surrounded at the time of his debut in the wilds of Ohio, his continued roughhousing in the dark down to our own days in essentially the same boisterous role (his last appearance in print is dated 1930 at Dr. Glen Hamilton's circle in Winnipeg) argue well for viewing him as the archetype of the spirit guide that produces seance room phenomena of a violent order with the touch of a master's hand.

The big question is: could this archetype attain to an independent psychic life as if born from the spiritualistic group, as if it were the child of the seance room, a kind of psychic homunculus? As he is not met with outside the seance room, privately as it were, but only manifests himself in the presence of entranced mediums, the answer is that his psychic life must be dependent on the group, that it has a functional, phenomenal being only, never quite the same and always dependent for color and character on the total personality of the parent medium. That would explain, without invoking illusion or fraud, why the various sketches and descriptions of him never agreed.

It also solves another perplexity: that he should have been so proficient in producing transportation phenomena with Herne and Williams, and unable to perform the same feat with many of his later proteges. Obviously if Herne and Williams possessed in abundance something which is necessary for a fourth-dimensional function, John King needed only to wave a magic wand and, presto, they were shuttling back and forth through the ceiling, while others, shut off from the same organismic power, were unable to loosen their ties to conventional space. This may be the key to the mystery of "conditions" regarding which John and Katie King never could give more than a nebulous answer.

As God created man male and female, man could be expected to generate a female companion, a daughter if not a wife, to his creation, the archetype. We first hear of Katie King in the seances of the Davenport Brothers, and in a not very complimentary fashion. Robert Cooper, describing a conversation between the spirits and the Davenports, writes in his biography:

> The next minute a shrill female voice was heard immediately in front of us. It was like that of a person of the lower walks of life and talked away, like many persons do, for the mere sake of talking. It was intimated that it was "Katie" who was speaking. There was a great attempt on her part at being witty, but according to my ideas on such matters, most of what was said would come under the category of small – very small – wit.

In another passage he writes:

> Unlike John, Katie will talk any length of time, as long in fact as she can find anything to talk about, even if it be the most frivolous nonsense; but I must do her the justice to say that she talks sensibly enough at times, and I have heard great wisdom in her utterances, and satisfactory answers given to profound philosophical questions.

Katie had no choice in the matter of parentage. If John King was a buccaneer, she was the buccaneer's daughter. So we find handed out to Crookes, in his famous seances with Florence Cook, the story that her name was Annie Owen Morgan; that she was about 12 years old when Charles I was beheaded; that she was married, had two children and committed many crimes, murdering people with her own hands; and that she died quite young, at the age of 22 or 23. She said that her attachment to Florence Cook served the purpose of convincing the world of the truth of Spiritualism and that this work was given her on the other side as a service to expiate her sins.

Florence Cook first met Katie in the seances of Herne and Williams when she was a mere child. Apparently Katie made a hit with her, as after a few years of incubation we find her manifesting herself in the Cook household when Florence was only 15 years old. The improvement in the Herne and Williams performance soon was noticeable. She was seen in materialized form, a Katie reborn. We are told that she was seen almost daily, the first time in April, 1872, showing a death-like face between the curtains. Later her materializations became more perfect, but it was only after a year of experimental work that she could walk out of the cabinet and show herself in full figure to the sitters. She was a nearly permanent inhabitant of the Cook household, walked about the house, appeared at unexpected moments, and went to bed with the medium, much to her annoyance. When Florence married, complications arose. According to Florence Marryat, Capt. Corner felt at first as if he had married two women and was not quite sure which of the two was his wife.

According to all accounts Katie was a beautiful girl. Crookes had 40 flashlight photographs of her. In most of them she noticeably resembles Miss Cook, but Crookes had no doubt of her independent identity. He writes:

> Photography was inadequate to depict the perfect beauty of Katie's face, as words are powerless to describe her charms of manner. Photography may, indeed, give a map of her countenance; but how can it reproduce the brilliant purity of her complexion, or the ever varying expression of her most mobile features, now overshadowed with sadness when relating some of the bitter experiences of her past life, now smiling with all the innocence of happy girlhood when she had collected my children round her, and was amusing them by recounting anecdotes of her adventures in India?

This is the Katie previous to the marriage of Florence Cook, and the lifelike materializations of which Crookes wrote so lyrically occurred, on this occasion, in his own house where Katie behaved like a human being of flesh and blood. It is one of the oddest and most unbelievable stories in Spiritualism: the greatest physicist of the last century as the recipient of revelations from the spirit world through a young girl who could become two persons, one more incredible than the other.

The last recorded appearance of Katie King, like that of John, her piratical parent, also was at Dr. Glen Hamilton's circle in Winnipeg in October, 1930, through the mediums Marie M. and Mercedes. In the words of the doctor:

> Obviously it is wholly impossible to say whether or not this Mary M.-Mercedes-Katie King is the same being as the entity appearing in the experiments of Crookes and others. We have the word of the controls in this case that it is so, and we have seen how, so far, these controls have repeatedly established the fact that they know whereof they speak . . . . While there are, I may say, some points of similarity to be traced between Katie as photographed by Crookes and Katie as photographed in the Winnipeg experiments, both faces for instance being rather long in formation, the eyes in both being large and luminous, the angle of the jaw in both being rather pronounced, the later Katie is so much younger in appearance, her beauty so much more apparent that it is evident that we cannot use the earlier record of her presence in any way as conclusive proof that there is any connection between the two.

Accepting Katie as the female archetype of the spirit guide, we would look only for functional and not bodily identity. An archetype could assume a thousand shapes and have none of its own.

But what of transportations where there was no spiritualistic circle, no archetype to rely upon?

We may assume that in such cases transportation was very rare and by no means recurrent. The spiritualist circle, however, is not the only aggregation that would favor an archetypal manifestation. The putative Sabbath to which the witches believed themselves transported by satanic agency was a similar, though imaginative, association with a group animated by identical beliefs. In a secret fraternity the power of ideology may be more potent as a binding force than in a private gathering of people with a common interest in psychic phenomena. Fairies dancing in a ring around a person sleeping on a fairy mound is another legendary combination suitable for archetypal manifestations. Let us not dismiss fairy belief too lightly. It was a very potent force in medieval England and, if transportation of human beings was ever a fact, fairies — as a shape for archetypal power — were just as capable of accomplishing it as the Devil or the spirits of the dead.

Having reduced spirits to archetypes, it now becomes clearer that the agency in transportation may be some mysterious fourth-dimensional function of human beings themselves, although as a rule in conjunction with the mediumistic talent. We may find a clue to this mysrious function in the ever-present condition of trance that precedes transportation.

What is trance? Let us say first what it is not. It is not a brown study, a spell, a day dream, an inspirational frenzy, ordinary or hypnotic sleep. We know what it is not but we do not know what it is, except that it is a distinct state of unconsciousness with marked physiological and psychological characteristics. The best way to obtain a glimpse of its true nature is to study the statements of those who experienced it. As it is the mediums who have most to say on the subject, I shall quote some of their testimonies and the observations of their investigators from my *Encyclopaedia of Psychic Science,* pp. 380-91:

D. D. Home testified before the London Dialectical Society:*

> I feel for two or three minutes in a dreamy state, then I become quite dizzy, and then I lose all consciousness. When I awake I find my feet and limbs cold, and it is difficult to restore the circulation. When told of what has taken place during the trance it is quite unpleasant to me, and I ask

*Established in 1867 to investigate the phenomena alleged to be Spiritual Manifestations, and "to report thereon." The report was privately printed in 1871. See *Encyclopaedia of Psychic Science,* pp. 88-89.

> those present not to tell me at once when I awake. I myself doubt what they tell me.

Lord Adare, speaking of Home's trance state, said:

> The change which takes place in him is very striking; he becomes, as it were, a being of higher type. There is a union of sweetness, tenderness and earnestness in his voice and manner which is very attractive.

Stainton Moses added these observations:

> By degrees Mr. Home's hands and arms began to twitch and move involuntarily. I should say that he has been partly paralyzed, drags one of his legs, moves with difficulty, stoops and can endure very little physical exertion. As he passed into the trance state he drew power from the circle by extending his arms to them and mesmerizing himself. All these acts are involuntary. He gradually passed into the trance state, and rose from the table, erect and a different man from what he was. He walked firmly, dashed out his arms and legs with great power and passed round to Mr. Crookes. He mesmerized him, and appeared to draw power from him.

Eglinton said of his experiences:

> I seemed to be no longer of this earth. A most ecstatic feeling came over me, and I presently passed into trance.
> I feel a cold shivering – stated Mrs. Mellon – a sensation as of water running down my back, noise in my ears, and a feeling as if I were sinking down into the earth; then I lost consciousness.

> I feel – said Mrs. Piper – as if something were passing over my brain, making it numb; a sensation similar to that experienced when I was etherised, only the unpleasant odour of the ether is absent. I feel a little cold, too, not very just a little, as if a cold breeze passed over me, and people and objects become smaller until they finally disappear; then, I know nothing more until I wake up, when the first things I am conscious of is a bright, a very bright light, and then darkness, such darkness. My

> hands and arms begin to tingle just as one's foot tingles after it has been "asleep," and I see, as if from a great distance, objects and people in the room; but they are very small and very black.

This agrees with the statements of the Seeress of Prevorst; waking from trance, the persons around her looked so thick and heavy that she could not imagine how they could move.*

It is quite important to quote from among Mrs. Piper's mumbled remarks during her return to consciousness: "I came in on a cord, a silver cord." Before she became conscious she heard a snap, sometimes two. They were physiological experiences. She said: ". . . sounds like wheels clicking together and then snaps."

Professor James found Mrs. Piper's lips and tongue insensible to pain while she was in trance. Dr. Hodgson later confirmed this by placing a spoonful of salt in Mrs. Piper's mouth. He also applied strong ammonia to the nostrils. Drastic experiments also were tried. Prof. James made a small incision in Mrs. Piper's left wrist. During trance the wound did not bleed and no notice was taken of the action. It bled freely afterwards and the medium bore the scar for life. In England Prof. Lodge pushed a needle suddenly into her hand. At another time Prof. Richet inserted a feather up her nostril. Harsh experiments in 1909 resulted in a badly blistered, swollen tongue which caused the medium inconvenience for several days, while another test resulted in numbness and partial paralysis of her right arm for some time.

The trance of Eusapia Paladino is described thus by Lombroso:

> At the beginning of the trance her voice is hoarse and all the secretions – sweat, tears, even the men-

*Justinus Kerner, M.D.: *The Seeress of Prevorst,* London, 1845.

strual secretion – are increased. Hyperaesthesia is succeeded by anaesthesia. Reflex movement of the pupils and tendons is lacking. Respiratory movement grows less frequent, passing from 18 inspirations to 15-12 a minute, heartbeats increase from 70-90-120. The hands are seized with jerkings and tremors. The joints of the feet and hands take on movement of flexure or extension, and every little while become rigid. The passing from this stage to that of active somnambulism is marked by yawns, sobs, perspiration on the forehead, passing of insensible perspiration through the skin of the hands, strange physiognomic expressions. Now she seems a prey to a kind of anger, expressed by imperious commands and sarcastic and critical phrases, and now to a state of voluptuous erotic ecstasy. She becomes pale, turns her eyes upward and her sight inward and exhibits many of the gestures that are frequent in hysterical fits. Towards the end of the trance when the more important phenomena occur she falls into true convulsions and cries like a woman who is lying-in, or else falls into profound sleep while from the aperture of the parietal bone in her head there exhales a warm fluid or vapour, sensible to the touch. After the seance she is overcome by morbid sensitiveness, hyperaesthesy, photophoby and often by hallucinations and delirium (during which she asks to be watched from harm) and by serious disturbances of the digestion, followed by vomiting if she has eaten before the seance; finally by true paresis of the legs, on account of which it is necessary for her to be carried and to be undressed by others. These disturbances are much aggravated if she is exposed to unexpected light.

The Italian Salvioli noticed for the first time that in trance the flow of blood to the brain is greater than in the waking state, consequently there is a greater physical activity and an increase in muscular excitability.

Prof. Flournoy frequently found complete allochiry, a confusion between the right and left side, with Mlle. Helen Smith. She would, in trance, consistently look for her pocket on the left side instead of on the right. If one of her fingers were pricked or pinched, it was the corresponding finger on the other hand which was agitated. Allochiry is one of the symptoms of hysteria.

Lombroso called attention to the fact that Eusapia Paladino, who usually was left-handed in sittings, became right-handed in one seance and Morselli himself became left-handed. This confirms Dr. Audenino's hypothesis of transitory left-handedness in the abnormal state, and the transference to the sitter of the anomalies of the medium. The left-handedness seems to indicate the increased participation of the right lobe of the brain in mediumistic states.

Prof. Morselli measured the left-handedness of Eusapia Paladino in dynamometric figures. He found, after a seance, a diminution of six kilograms for the right and 14 for the left hand. The spirits of Mrs. Piper always communicated on the left side. The trance, as a rule, begins with hissing intakes of breath and ends with deep expirations. There is a suggestion in it of the Yoga system of breathing. "Like the fakirs," wrote Morselli, "when they wish to enter into trance, Eusapia begins to slacken her rate of breathing." Swedenborg believed that his powers were connected with a system of respiration. He said that in communing with the spirits he hardly breathed for half an hour at a time.

These are exceedingly interesting and provoking statements and observations.

I will now quote from the *Encyclopaedia of Psychic Science,* p. 179, on the relationship of the hypnotic to the mediumistic trance:

"The first essential difference is that the mediumistic trance is voluntary and self-induced, though hypnotism, for the purpose of relieving the medium of the attendant physiological suffering, is sometimes employed to bring it about. Dr. Ochorowitz saved Mlle. Tomczyk much exhaustion by hypnotizing her. Mme. Bisson similarly facilitated the materialization phenomena of Eva C. Kathleen Goligher was hypnotized by Dr. Crawford, the Didier Brothers were always accompanied by a magnetizer and the mediumship of Andrew Jackson Davis was initiated by hypnotic clairvoyance. Generally, if the hypnotized subject is a medium, he exhibits faculties of a far more transcendental character than ordinary subjects. Ordinary faculties of clairvoyance will progress to travelling clairvoyance and it is very likely that many of the wonderful phenomena of early mesmerizers was due to the fact that their subjects, unknown to them, were mediums.

"The hypnotized subject has great powers of personation. But he does not claim, unless so suggested, communication with the dead. In the mediumistic trance such suggestion does not work. Those whose appearance is yearned for often do not communicate at all, many strangers come and go and all the controls exhibit a distinct personality far surpassing in variety the imitative efforts of any hypnotized subject. If they were subjective creations of the medium's mind they would not exhibit these special peculiarities by which the sitters establish their identity with their departed friends. The hypnotic self is sincere and does not exhibit such diabolic cunning as the personation of hundreds of individuals and the acquisition of facts deeply buried in the subconscious or totally unknown to the sitters.

"The hypnotic personality has an uncanny sense of time. The spirit controls, on the other hand, are very vague and uncertain on this point. Their messages are not exactly located in time, and are sometimes borne out by past or near future happenings.

"Professor William James made many attempts to see whether Mrs. Piper's medium-trance had any community of nature with ordinary hypnotic trance. The first two attempts to hypnotize her failed but after the fifth attempt she had become a pretty good hypnotic subject 'as far as muscular phenomena and automatic imitations of speech and gesture go; but I could not affect her consciousness, or otherwise get her beyond this point. Her condition in this semi-hypnosis is very different from her medium-trance. The latter is characterized by great muscular unrest, even her ears moving vigorously in a way impossible to her in her waking state, but in hypnosis her muscular relaxation and weakness are extreme. She often makes several efforts to speak before her voice becomes audible; and to get a strong contraction of the hand, for example, express manipulation and suggestion must be practised. Her pupils contract in the medium-trance. Suggestions to the control that he should make her recollect after the medium-trance what she had been saying were accepted, but had no result. In the hypnotic trance such a suggestion will often make the patient remember all that has happened.' "

Let us now turn to ecstasy. Here we have to tread warily. Catholic writers have put an immense effort into showing that the ecstasy of the saints has nothing in common with mediumistic trance, that the latter is diabolical, while the former is divine. They describe ecstasy an "an alienation of all sensitive life, or life of relation, as though the soul were no longer in the body,* and divide it into three stages: ecstasy properly so-called, rap-

*Mgr. Albert Farges: *Mystical Phenomena,* Burns, Oates & Washburne, London, 1926, p. 163.

ture and the flight of the spirit. This is how St. Teresa of Avila, the famous reformer of the Carmelite Order distinguishes the shades of difference:

" '1. In ordinary ecstasy, the suspension of the powers in God takes place tranquilly, with a gentle and calm sweetness, like a sort of flowing of the soul into the bosom of divinity: thus mystics have often called it by the name of flowing or liquefaction. It might be compared to an overflowing or deliquescence of the soul, which seems to abandon its own life in order to be blended and lost in the ocean of life divine. . . .

" '2. Rapture, as its name denotes, is always impetuous. The soul does not seem to animate the body. . . . A rapture is absolutely irresistible, whilst Union, inasmuch as we are still on our own ground, may be hindered, though that resistance be painful and violent; it is, however, almost always impossible. But rapture, for the most part, is irresistible. It comes, in general, as a shock, quick and sharp, before you can collect your thoughts or help yourself in any way, and you seem and feel it as a cloud or strong eagle rising upwards and carrying you away on its wings.

" 'I repeat it; you feel and see yourself carried away, you know not whither. For though we feel how ridiculous it is, yet the weakness of our nature makes us afraid at first, and we require a much more resolute and courageous spirit, than in the previous states, in order to risk everything, come what may, and to abandon ourselves into the hands of God, and to go willingly whither we are carried, seeing that we must be carried away, however painful it may be. And so strong is it, that I would very often resist and exert all my strength, particularly at those times when the rapture was coming upon me in public. I did so, too, very often, when I was alone, because I was afraid of delusions. Occasionally, I was able, by great efforts, to make a slight resistance; but afterwards I was worn out, like a person who had been contending with a strong giant; at other times it was impossible to resist at all; my soul was carried away, and almost always my head with it – and now and then the whole body as well, so that it was lifted up from the ground. . . .

" 'When the rapture was over, my body seemed frequently to be buoyant, as if all weight had departed from it; so much so that now and then I scarcely knew that my feet touched the ground.

" '3. The flight of the spirit is a rapture of special intensity which throws the mind into a stupor and thrill of wonderment. The soul seems to separate itself from the body and to take its flight toward its blessed home.' "

The distinction between the second and third stage is a rather delicate one, and the psychological experience itself is identical to the cosmic consciousness described by Dr. R. M. Bucke without the necessary status of sainthood. It is a consciousness of the cosmos, of the life and order of the universe. It is considered a higher, yet at present exceptional peak of human evolution which the race will universally attain in a distant future. . . . The experience comes suddenly without warning, with a sensation of being immersed in a flame or rose-colored cloud and is accompanied by a feeling of ecstasy, moral and intellectual illumination in which, like a flash, a clear conception in outline is presented to the mind of the meaning and drift of the universe. The man who goes through the experience sees and knows that the cosmos is a living presence, that life is eternal, the soul of man immortal, that the foundation principle of the world is love and that the happiness of every individual in the long run is absolutely certain. He loses all fear of death, all sense of sin, his personality gains added charm and he becomes transfigured. In a few moments of the experience he will learn more than in months or years of study, and will learn much that no study can teach.*

Let us now turn our attention to the physiology of transportation as we have no accounts of mental experiences during the actual vanishing and reappearance. It is quite possible that there is a mental correspondence to the instantaneous physical flight through space, but the shock of the experience produces complete amnesia, an outstanding physiological symptom in itself.

Other signs that the transported persons are in a state of deep shock is the feeling of exhaustion, trembling and crying which they evidence on recovering consciousness. Herne complained of a violent heartbeat and thirst, Lottie Fowler had a rapid and fluttering pulse, Eglinton moaned because the back of his head hurt, Miller had a pain in the heart, Henderson was bathed in perspiration, Mrs. Salmon spat blood, Mrs. Guppy and the Marquis Centurione Scotto felt they must have gone mad and even the dogs that came as apports during the former's seances yelped and barked throughout the evening, indicating an excited mental state.

The sick feeling before and the dazed condition after the experience seems to be a general symptom. Here and there we have hints that too sudden awakening after transportation is dangerous, that both body and mind need some time for recovery,** but it is rather surpris-

Encyclopaedia of Psychic Science, p. 65.
**Even the butterflies of Mrs. Guppy appeared dazed and inanimate on their arrival.

ing how short this period of recovery is. The longest sleep on record is only two and a half hours by Marquis Centurione Scotto in the hayloft of the Millesimo stables. As we have no record of fatalities, we can only view the mechanics of the phenomenon with amazement.

◀ CHAPTER XIX ▶

Needs and Power

WHAT GOOD does human transportation serve, if any?

Charles Fort suggested that transportation may be a means employed by Nature to distribute things over the face of the earth, human beings getting entangled presumably by accident. It is a fascinating idea but it savors of the *Erd Geist,* the belief in which is a relic of past ages of thought. An alternate suggestion on similar lines could be offered by picturing Nature as a vast machinery and man as the spanner which, through some twist in his mental processes, accidentally falls into the works, transportation being a kind of instantaneous protective elimination. But such romantic ideas will not bring us nearer to the heart of the problem.

Logical consideration demands that we should approach it from two fundamental angles: is human transportation accidental or purposive? Do some people fall through a hole in space by rare chance, or does it happen through conscious or unconscious planning?

If it is accidental, our line of inquiry is closed until we find out more of the strange world in which we live. If it is purposive, we have two sub-questions: (1) is the purpose resident in an agency outside the individual, or (2) is it resident solely or by the greatest measure within him?

The case of Habakkuk illustrates a belief in the highest possible outside agency: God. The very description: caught up by the Spirit of the Lord, as found in the Bible, suggests that, from the religious approach, transportation is a miracle, a manifestation of the power and purpose of God; and that is all there is to it. Such humble acceptances do not satisfy the scientific mind. We see the purpose in Habakkuk's transportation: to feed Daniel with pottage — a rather shabby provender from and a doubtful device of the Lord. Why Elijah was carried to Heaven in a chariot of fire is not even intimated. No design is shown behind Philip's strange leap through space. The case of the man Paul knew is more than dubious; a revelation which is not revealed (unspeakable words. . .not lawful to utter) is not even paradoxical.

Descending lower in the spiritual hierarchy in search for purpose, we meet the Devil and his minions, then the fairies, the Poltergeist, the ghost of the haunted house and the spirits of the dead. Finally, at the bottom rung of the ladder, we find our very human magician. They are all outside agents whose stock is rather low, the spirit guide shining as the most down-to-earth party. Once, however, we reduce the latter to an archetype, we deprive him of an independent psychic life and transform him, more or less, into a creation of the unconscious. The Poltergeist and the ghost of the haunted house as possible archetypes of malice and evil conscience might yield their secrets to a similar approach.

If the agency of transportation resides in the individual we are faced with the question: what are *his* motives? Random acts, chance or coincidence may well conceal an unconscious purpose. If we can find that purpose, we clarify the psychological picture.

As motives and purposes are more descriptive of conscious manifestations, let us talk of needs and reword our query: what are the needs of the unconscious that transportation alone can satisfy?

Obviously, the need of self-preservation must stand out foremost. We find two instances where this motive is discernible. Mrs. Barkel was hit by a car, or about to be hit, and in that instant she found herself recovering at a distance which could not have been covered by any reflex jump. She claimed at least that it was a case of transportation and that it saved her life. D. D. Home had a similar experience but his claim is levitation, not transportation. As transportation was an unknown phenomenon in his mediumship, whereas levitation stood out as his principal feat, and as his tremendous narcissism prevented him from believing in any mediumistic phenomenon he himself could not produce, we shall accept his story as a second best illustration. We may suspect the same need of life preservation behind other instances where no conscious awareness of a deadly danger existed. As a matter of fact, only an unconscious intimation of the danger may have the power to release the trigger for the dynamics of transportation to become operative.* This is why the disappearance of Apollonius while on trial before Domitian is inherently unlikely.

Saving somebody else's life might be an unconscious need almost as powerful as self-preservation. We have the story of St. Anthony whose transportation (back and forth between Lisbon and Padua) had the avowed purpose of saving his father who was on trial before the Court. A physician may be "moved" by similar needs.

*"When something injurious has insidious designs on the organism, the latter . . . awaits motionless and deathly still for what is going to happen. It makes itself resemble and be identical with the surrounding physical world. (Mimicry) . . . Every trauma still evokes that old fantasy pattern of camouflage, of disappearing in the universe." Dr. A. M. Meerloo, "Shock — A Psychosomatic Phenomenon," *Journal of Nervous and Mental Disease,* June, 1950.

Such is the report about Apollonius of Tyana who was wanted at Ephesus when the plague broke out in that town and was immediately there. If we forget about the voice of the Lord, Habakkuk went to the rescue of Daniel inspired by similar ideals of service.

For the saints, saving somebody's soul was more important than saving mere physical life. We find this need operative in the story of Mary of Agreda who is said to have made 500 mysterious visits through space from Spain across the ocean to the savages of Mexico.

Self-preservation must not be restricted to the danger of death. One may die worse than physical death through mental agony. The need of escape from a given unbearable situation may be as strong as saving one's life. The saints will escape through religion to Heaven whether transported or levitated. For Joseph of Copertino levitation was sufficient and only incidental. He reached God, like so many other saints, through ecstasies — a perfect compensation for his dreary and unsatisfactory life. The Marquis Centurione Scotto had a broken heart over the death of his son. Only a stupendous psychic manifestation could finally lay his doubts regarding an afterlife. So he vanished from a circle of his friends.

But what about the average man who knows of no religious or psychic solution to an unendurable life? Must he just die?

Here is a story by Arthur Lambton, a noted London personality, one of the founders of the London Crime Club, which I copy from the *Daily Mail,* August 9, 1935:

"In the year 1768 there resided at Shepton Mallet, in Somerset, an ex-sailor named Owen Parfitt. He was paralysed, and was looked after by his sister. It was his habit when the weather was fine to sit in front of his cottage door wrapped up in an overcoat while his sister busied herself within and chatted with him. This is what happened on the evening of June 6. When she failed to receive any reply to one of her questions his sister stepped out — to find no trace of the paralytic except the overcoat.

"To make the episode still more bizarre the adjoining field was full of haymakers. Yet that was the last that was ever seen of Parfitt. So things ran until November 1813, when a labourer digging 150 yards from the cottage unearthed a human head and a skeleton. And so at last the mystery was in a way said to be solved.

"But then came the report of the anatomist from Bristol proving the remains to be feminine beyond doubt. And so once more the legend was renewed that Owen Parfitt had been spirited away by the devil, for in his youth he was said to have been involved in both the white and the black slave traffic in Africa."

For a paralyzed man, tied to a wheelchair, life may become unendurable. At least in one instance we have seen a man cured of psychosis by suddenly being lifted in the air. He was Baldassar Rossi with whom Joseph of Copertino ascended, after grabbing him by a lock of his hair. Transportation also may act as a shock therapy. If that was the way Parfitt disappeared, did he land on the Dark Continent to which he was tied by the contents of his unconscious, and what happened to him thereafter? It is anybody's guess.

Purely egotistic and manic needs are discernible behind witchcraft and magical stories of transportation. The drive for power by the so-called witches must have been of tremendous intensity. They were willing to die on the pyre for their faith in a nether world. We can consider it as a considerable cultural achievement that the psychic stream running through dark byways of the mind has been domesticated and trained to flow through spiritualistic channels instead of pursuing the course of traditional black magic. That is why we have no witches and magicians today.

It takes a poet to be transported to Fairyland and to win a Fairy Queen. Thomas the Rhymer is said to have accomplished the deed. This is a libidinal triumph, as such dominated by the need of race preservation, but in the particular form it takes by the journey to Fairyland it is a regressive phenomenon, a fantasy of return into the uterus.

From this emerges a novel angle for approaching the problem of the energy by which human transportation is accomplished. As the unborn lives in a watery universe of its own in which gravitation is partly annulled, levitation is a near parallel to the floating of the fetus in the amniotic fluid, while transportation is a sudden magical re-attainment of the fetal estate.

Would the fetus exist not only psychologically but literally at the center of the universe, it would be entirely free of gravitation. We may take a cosmic view of conception by borrowing from the Biblical narrative of creation and say that the Spirit of God moves over the face of the waters whenever a child is conceived! Assuredly, the same spirit that built the universe is responsible for the creation of a child, the parents blindly obeying Nature's demand. Creation is inconceivable without energy, and energy is one of the ultimate things of which we know nothing, observing its manifestation only. That it is subservient to the life force, we may gather whenever the so-called mitogenic force of a frail mushroom lifts and splits a heavy block of marble which bars its access to light and air. Would not the far more complex system of the fetus be possessed of a similar and even greater power?

It is a permissible speculation that, in a vestigial form, an electromagnetic power is hidden in the organism of the adult body. This is the only power that could accomplish the stupendous feat of human transportation. It needs the condition of trance or ecstasy for its liberation, presumably because these states are the nearest parallels to the physiological and psychological status of the unborn. When the power is freed, it counteracts gravitation as in levitation, or affects space as in transportation. Sometimes this effect on space may be due to a blind discharge of fetal energies, at other times the power may well up in answer to tremendous unconscious needs.